BOOKS BY DAVID HAPGOOD

AFRICA: FROM INDEPENDENCE
TO TOMORROW   *1965*

AFRICA *(in the series* TODAY'S WORLD IN FOCUS)   *1965*

AFRICA: FROM INDEPENDENCE
TO TOMORROW

AFRICA:

DAVID HAPGOOD

From Independence to Tomorrow

Atheneum NEW YORK *1965*

For Janice

Contents

Preface

How can we understand Africa? The news from that continent is often bewildering, and the literature on Africa, though increasingly abundant, rarely helps the reader who does not propose to make its study his life work. Few of us have time to plow through the valuable but narrow work of specialists, and the more general writings are all too often emptily superficial, irrelevant or patronizing.

My aim here is to set down, briefly and I hope clearly, what is important about the new Africa. The book presents a thesis, a way of seeing Africa, that runs counter to conventional thinking. It is a book of people and situations, not statistics. Enough background is included so that it can be read by anyone with a general knowledge of recent history, and those who want to know the populations and presidents of African nations can find this information in any of several recent almanac-style reference books. My focus is on Africa itself, not on the cold war or on "what they think of us"; those who would like to hear what the State Department should do in this week's African crisis must look elsewhere (though I believe American policy would be sounder if based on the realities described here). I am writing for the readers who ask something like this: "What are the Africans doing now that they're independent? What do the people need and how can they get it? Why do things happen the way they do?" The book provides a framework of related ideas that help to answer those questions.

"You can't generalize about Africa" is the immediate objection, and in the text I criticize the instant experts who tell Africans what to do the same day they get off the plane. Africa has too much variety to permit generalization, it will be said; there are at least eight hundred distinct cultures in the region covered here. It is even hard to generalize about a single nation. What can we say, for example, about Kenya, where two such different peoples as the Kikuyu and the Masai live side by side? What can we say about how "Kenyans" think or work or love? Fortunately, in each of the topics we shall take up, there is much unity under Africa's multifaceted variety. Most of those eight hundred cultures have many basic traits in common; man's relationship to the land, for example, is similar almost everywhere. The impact of colonial rule was similar, too, all over Africa, and in fact there are many analogies between what has happened in Africa and the clash between Western and traditional civilizations in other parts of the world. Improving the conditions of life in Africa will require an endless variety of local techniques, but the principles guiding those techniques are the same in most cases.

This book is not about all of Africa. It does not include the Berber-Arab nations of northern Africa or the white-ruled regions of southern Africa. It is about independent black Africa, or central or tropical or sub-

Saharan Africa, as it is variously called. When I write "Africa," that is what I mean, with apologies to the Atlas.

The points of view set forth here are, I believe, valid for all that broad area whose people number about two hundred million, though again local variations on the theme are infinite. The book is the result of nearly two years spent in Africa, and another year of study in the United States and France; in 1964 I made two trips back to Africa. Though the thesis is general, the illustrations and anecdotes are mostly taken from the places where we spent the most time. For one school year, we—a family of four—lived in Dakar, Senegal, where our sons attended the Lycée Delafosse. The following year my wife and I traveled through thirteen nations of West and East Africa. There are large areas of Africa that we did not visit, but we traveled in and studied every major zone.

The father of the book is Richard H. Nolte, director of the Institute of Current World Affairs, though he is of course not responsible for his offspring's conduct. We went to Africa on a fellowship from the Institute, and the support and encouragement of Mr. Nolte and the Institute staff sustained us through our long journey of discovery and self-discovery (for, as Mr. Nolte knows, the study of another people is also a study of one's self). My wife, Janice, is in a true sense my co-author. The "we" is not an editorial we: without Janice's deep and humane perceptions, I would have learned far less than I did, and without her infallible sense of direction I probably would not have found my way home again. I am a reporter by trade, and in combining elements from several academic disciplines I have borrowed from specialists too numerous to list. Those who know their thinking will recognize how much I owe to Ben Mady Cissé, Director of *Animation* in Senegal, to René Dumont, the agronomist, and to Louis-Joseph Lebret, the planner. My fellows at the Massachusetts Institute of Technology Summer Study Conference on Agricultural Productivity will observe what those fruitful six weeks contributed to my knowledge. But the synthesis of ideas is my own, and naturally I claim credit for whatever errors the book contains.

Overwhelmingly, my greatest debt is to the people of Africa. Most of my ideas and information came from them, and, more important, we owe a personal debt that we can never repay. We loved Africa and its people. During the two years that we wandered the continent, we were received with unfailing warmth and hospitality, even in places and by people reputedly "antiforeign" or "anti-American." In remote villages around a kerosene lamp, along dusty roads and in air-conditioned urban palaces, Africans of all classes—poor and rich, illiterate and intellectual—gave us generously of their time and of themselves. Once human contact was established, Africans told us about their lives with honesty and depth of feeling; and I hope we did the same. Details stick in the memory. One man, father-in-law of a friend, took two days of his life to guide us through a particularly difficult stretch of bush; we'll never forget that, nor a dozen incidents like it. Many Africans not overly fond of our race did us the honor, too rare in this world, of judging us as individuals, not as stereotypes. Of our generous welcome all over black Africa, a white American can only say that we deserved much less than we were given.

To the African people then, and especially to the hundreds who helped us along our way, I apologize for whatever may be offensive in this book. Much of what I say is harshly critical of those now in power (though in no way a defense of the departed colonial rulers) and the book is far from optimistic. Some of those I criticize are friends of ours; I hope they will still be our friends. These criticisms were first voiced to me by Africans, not by Old Africa Hands clustered around hotel bars. Many Africans who might be expected to be on the defensive are courageously free in their self-criticism—more free, in fact, than most of their foreign friends. I fervently believe that the truth should be told about Africa, if we are ever to understand the painful inner conflicts that must be resolved before Africans can achieve the richer life that all men deserve. It is in the interest of the people of Africa that this book was conceived and written.

AFRICA: FROM INDEPENDENCE
TO TOMORROW

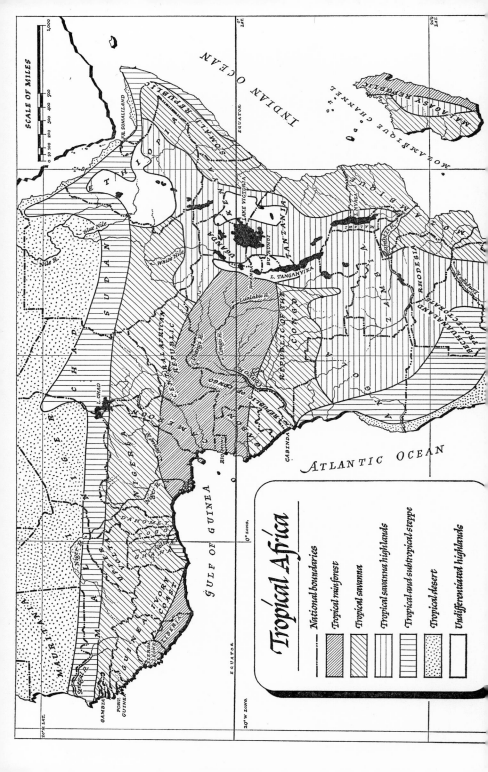

CHAPTER ONE

Strands of the Web

Most Africans live by farming. If we are interested in the future of Africa, we must understand what kind of world they live in. To achieve a better material life, African farmers must adopt a whole set of new techniques, and for this to happen, millions of people living in isolation from the urban centers must decide they want to make revolutionary changes in their lives. Agricultural progress does not begin and end with a new tool or a different crop, for the way men work cannot be separated from other aspects of their lives. Agriculture is interwoven into the patterns of African society. Change in how a man farms his land means change in how he thinks about land and farming, and change in how he views the world and himself in relation to other men. The essential change lies in the idea of change itself: the idea that man can better control his environment, and that it is worth sacrificing custom handed down for centuries in order to live better.

Progress in rural Africa, therefore, depends on profound changes in the attitudes and ways of living of

3

millions of villagers. But not on them alone. The new technology will be funneled through the tiny educated class that holds power in the capitals of independent Africa. Far more than in Western nations, especially the United States, the responsibility for progress rests on the state. If roads are to be built, research on new crops sponsored and then put to use, farm credit systems set up and honestly administered, the ruling elites must start the process. The attitudes of the elite, the values that guide their decisions, are as important as those of rural Africans, for the elite too must innovate. Do they want rural progress, if the price is change in their own way of life? The question applies to presidents and peasants alike.

If the elite really wants progress, then its members must be able to communicate with the farmers. Communication is essential to rural development. An industrial project like, say, a bauxite mine, can be built in one place with few employees, using well-known techniques and, perhaps, foreign aid and experts. Not so in agriculture. Agricultural progress requires reaching those scattered millions of farmers and adapting any new technology to a great variety of local conditions. Reaching the rural people is not easy. African states are of course poor in skilled manpower; they do not have a fraction of the numbers needed to man the new services that go with a modernized agriculture. Africa needs "poor" methods of rural development: channels of communication that reach the greatest numbers at the least cost in skilled manpower.

A more subtle barrier to communication between rural farmers and the ruling elite lies in the vast gap in attitudes that separates the two. In most African nations, no one language is spoken by everyone or even a ma-

jority, but the problem is far deeper than that. When
we say that someone "doesn't talk my language," we
don't mean that the actual words are foreign, but that
the attitudes he holds are alien. The basic fact about
Africa today is the alienation between its two cultures:
peasants and presidents do not "talk the same language."
The peasant lives in that culture known as "traditional,"
the president in a culture best described as "colonial-
European." Both cultures are handed down from generation to generation by education, the process by which a
society teaches its children to hold the "right" values, to
think about the world in the way that society approves.
It is common today to speak of "education for development," as if any kind of schooling were valuable in itself.
Yet education is intrinsically neutral, a conveyor belt
whose utility depends on what is being transmitted. So
it is essential for us to know whether the content of
African education is suited to Africa's needs—whether it
makes communication and creative change easier or
more difficult.

To communicate, Africans must "talk the same language" in the deepest cultural sense. An African nation
needs a single culture shared by peasants and elite; we
will argue that neither traditional nor colonial-European
culture is likely to serve Africa's purposes. Innovation
requires people who are flexible, who have a taste for
change and experimentation. Since there is no blueprint
to be slavishly followed, such people must be confident
of their ability to take chances and win out. If they are to
believe they can master their environment, they must
believe in themselves and in their culture.

Every people needs to believe it is a "god-bearing
people," Dostoyevsky wrote. In order to mobilize the
energy and sacrifice needed for progress, a people must

believe in the special merit of their own civilization. (This faith need not be religious. It may be Communism, or it may be the democratic faith that inspires young Americans to give up their lives in Mississippi.) This issue underlies every other in Africa today. The old gods of Africa are dying, and the new gods are foreign. Caught between two worlds, one dying and the other alien, Africans are in danger of losing their souls: they do not seem to believe themselves a god-bearing people.

Agriculture, politics, education are all strands in a web at whose center lies Africa's quest for a new culture. None of these strands can be understood if viewed separately; it is the web of relations among them that gives them their meaning. A tug on one strand is immediately resisted in other strands whose position has been disturbed. The single-factor panaceas advanced every day for Africa—economic planning, foreign aid, cooperatives, the one-party state, and, above all, education—are dangerous oversimplifications, for they propose to pull on one strand of the web without taking the others fully into account. In examining the nature of the web that links agriculture, politics and education, we shall in turn take up the heritage of European rule, the nature of African traditional society, the performance of the ruling elites since independence, the record of African agriculture and its requirements for the future, two interesting experiments in rural development, the consequences of the present system of formal schooling, the continuing foreign involvement in Africa, and the university students who are the next generation of the elite. Finally, we shall inquire into how Africans are going about their search for a soul, and then we shall take a diffident look into the future.

Africa, like any other place, is people, not theories. The decisions of its obscure millions, not the planner at

his drawing board, will shape its future. Here, chosen
from the notebook of a traveler's memory, are some
vignettes that may convey something of the human atmosphere of the fascinating, contradictory world that is
Africa today.

In the deep bush of Senegal, an African governor takes
us with him on his first tour of the remote region that is
now his responsibility. The previous governor was
French. "I am black like you," the African governor
says to the peasants assembled to greet him in each village. But he cannot speak directly to his people. Born in
another region of Senegal, educated in French schools
and in France, the governor speaks none of the local
languages; so he speaks in French and an interpreter
translates his words—"I am black like you"—for the peasants. As we bounce in a Landrover over the dusty trails
between villages, the governor chats easily of French literature and quotes whole paragraphs of *Madame Bovary*.
He admits that he knows nothing of the culture of the
people he now governs; "I am seeing Africa for the first
time," he tells us. "We are the sacrificed generation,"
he says of his age group, educated Senegalese in their
mid-thirties—the road to his present position was not an
easy one. But the governor earns in a year what the peasant, black like him, earns in forty years, if he lives that
long, which is statistically unlikely. The governor has
lived in a time of bewilderingly rapid change: he has
been an African child in the heyday of colonial rule,
then a subordinate to the French in the evening of empire, and now governor in an independent nation.
"Things are different now," he tells his people, but for
the peasants virtually nothing has changed over the long
centuries.

*   *   *

7

The new Houphouet-Boigny bridge in Abidjan, capital of the Ivory Coast, makes a visitor wonder if he is in New Jersey rather than the new Africa. High fluorescent street lights shine on the approaches to the bridge. At night clusters of children gather under each light with their schoolbooks. It is the only place where they can read; there is no electricity in the nearby shantytown where they live.

The glittering white National Assembly building in Dakar, capital of Senegal, is one of the newest and grandest legislative buildings in the world. It was put up by the French, using the most modern construction techniques, just before Senegal became independent. In the Assembly, the deputies debate in French on the meaning of African socialism. Within the building's shadow, a barefoot laborer dressed in rags is clearing the brush that has overgrown an empty lot. The laborer uses a *daba,* a short-handled hoe that has not changed in millennia. He gathers the brush he has cleared piece by piece and carries it away by the handful. For the *daba* is his only tool: he has neither rake nor wheelbarrow.

In the deserts of Mauritania, which lies south of Morocco, a halfway house between Arab and Black Africa, nomads follow their herds in the endless search for water. Riding camels, with the wind billowing their flowing blue gowns, they look like figures from a Biblical scene; their way of life has changed little in two thousand years. We are sitting on rugs under a nomad's tent made of black skins, sipping camel's milk mixed with water and sugar from a wooden bowl. A Mauritanian asks us to please explain one clause in the Evian accord that had ended the war in Algeria. "I cannot understand

8

why the Algerians made those concessions," he comments, and it is soon clear that he knows the accord inside out. He and his clan have no experience of the world beyond their sands; they have never seen a city or green fields. But they do have a transistor radio. Leaping all natural barriers, the airwaves now bring them the winds of propaganda and information from every ideological point of the globe. Their knowledge is weirdly mixed. They do not know the many simple techniques that might improve their lives; but they know what men are saying in Washington, Moscow, Peking, London, Paris, Cairo.

In Niamey, the dusty sleepy little capital of Niger, a newly installed traffic light shines red. No cars are in sight; only a camel and his driver wait for the light to turn green.

The government of Upper Volta, landlocked and poor even by African standards, has decided to open an embassy in Japan, half a world away, and to install a television station in Ouagadougou, its capital. Television sets will sell for a price equal to what a peasant earns in three years, and the telecasts will reach only a small fraction of the nation's area. The government has also decreed an austerity campaign.

Two young men in a distant Senegalese town ask us for a lift to Dakar, the capital, two days' drive and a world away. They are shabbily dressed in clothes that are half African and half European, and they carry their belongings wrapped in a cloth. From their halting French, we guess that they attended a primary school for a few years but did not graduate. They tell us that they

9

are returning to their jobs in Dakar after a vacation at home. But when we reach the great city of Dakar, the two boys are unable to direct us among its huge buildings to where they say they live; it is soon obvious to us that they have never before been in Dakar. The address they gave us was surely that of relatives; but, without skills, the boys' chances of finding jobs are slim in a city overflowing with unemployed men. On the first day of the journey, we passed through a little village of thatched huts. The men were returning from the fields, and women dressed only in a wrap-around skirt were gracefully carrying firewood on their heads long miles to their homes. It was the dry season, so the wheels of our car threw dust in their faces; so rare are cars that a young girl panicked and dashed into the bush, scattering her bundle of wood. The peasants laughed and called greetings to us, as they do to any travelers whose passage briefly interrupts the monotony of their days. To our surprise, one of the youths in the car burst out, with a bitterness rare in soft-spoken Africa: "Look at those people—they're savages—they don't know anything." It is from "those people," from tradition-bound peasant life, that these two young men are fleeing, because they have been to school for a few years. For much the same motives, the government of Senegal has decreed that women must cover their breasts in public.

Mansour Gueye, government engineer, is an unusual personality among educated Africans. Caring little for clothes, he wears rumpled dusty khakis even on occasions when his fellow officials are nattily uniformed. Gueye is vigorous and impatient to get things done; he gives little time to the ceremonial greetings, the endless polite inquiries about the health of distant relatives, that pre-

cede most African conversations. He runs his office of
public works like an efficiency expert, and on his desk is
a sign: YOUR TIME IS PRECIOUS / MINE IS ALSO / BE BRIEF.
Gueye is stocky and very black, with quick humorous
eyes and breezy good nature. He seems more American
than African, except, of course, that he is a devout Muslim and has two wives. That day Gueye is addressing
about forty government employees at a meeting in a
rudimentary hall in a bush town. The meeting has been
dragging on through endless speeches and discussion.
Next to us a young man with a winning smile offers
cheerfully irrelevant comments in his soft African-
accented French. While engineer Gueye is speaking, he
is constantly interrupted by a clerk, known to all present
as half crazy, who makes vague accusations against
Gueye's department and launches into wild harangues
that seem to have no subject at all. Gueye controls himself far longer than would most Westerners, but at last
he loses his temper and says to the clerk: "If you don't
have anything to say on the subject, keep quiet or I'll
come down there and knock you flat." We are sympathetic, but the tone of the meeting turns, subtly and
unmistakably, against the engineer; he is gently chided
by one of the presiding officials. In African terms, Gueye
is in the wrong, for he has not let the clerk have his say,
no matter how pointless that say is, and so he has broken
the unity of the group. Later a young teacher struggles
to explain to us his feelings about Mansour Gueye. Of
course the clerk is crazy, and of course Gueye is doing a
great deal for the community. But somehow Gueye is
"not one of us." "He doesn't come to our meetings, and
he closes his door at night."

CHAPTER TWO

The Mask of Colonialism

Many Africans have commented on the surprises they encountered when they first went to Europe: the extraordinary sight of white men sweeping the streets is often mentioned. For the face of Europe-in-Africa was not the face of Europe itself: the productive, innovating, and relatively democratic air of Britain and France was absent in their colonies. This difference is essential to understanding what Europe actually has done to Africa. The face of Europe-in-Africa was a somnolent, lordly European surrounded by servile Africans. When independence came to Guinea, artists in the little town of Mamou pictured the past as a mustachioed Frenchman in colonial helmet and uniform, a sort of Gallic Colonel Blimp, with his wife riding in a sedan chair on the shoulders of her black servants.

The early conquerors were often colossal figures like Cecil Rhodes, full of vigor and imagination as well as greed. But once the colonies were peaceful, the opportunity to lord it over the Africans attracted the rejects of Europe, men who could not make their way in their own

society. (Much the same was true of the United States
and Latin America, as anyone can testify who has met
the Americans found on the plantations of the United
Fruit Company.) The picture in Mamou is of course
overdrawn: devoted and energetic Europeans could be
found in the colonial administration. But the environment pushed them in another direction, and the Europeans in Africa, like people anywhere, conformed to
their environment. A Malagasy lady said of French new-
comers to the island of Madagascar: "Often they are fine
when they arrive. But after six months they are as bad as
the rest." In his essay "Shooting an Elephant," George
Orwell, who was once a police officer in Burma, described how the colonial environment captured the men
who governed it: "I perceived in this moment that when
the white man turns tyrant it is his own freedom that he
destroys. He becomes a sort of hollow, posing dummy,
the conventionalized figure of a sahib. For it is the condition of his rule that he shall spend his life in trying to
impress the natives. . . . He wears a mask, and his face
grows to fit it."

The "mask" was that of a human being superior by
his birth: the European was compelled to "impress the
natives" with his own unique ability to rule. How else,
after all, could a tiny group of officials maintain their
alien rule over the African masses without the constant
and wasteful use of military force? Without a large
measure of consent on the part of the colonial peoples,
the empire became too expensive to be worth keeping—
as Gandhi proved in India.

To "impress the natives" with European superiority
meant also to impress them with African inferiority. The
belief that Africans were "primitive savages" incapable
of governing themselves was a necessary part of the

mythology of imperialism. "Africans are like children," the French said, and Trollope wrote of African man: "No approach to the civilization of his white fellow creatures, whom he imitates as a monkey does a man." The myth helped excuse the excesses of colonial rule: If the Africans were exploited and occasionally ill-treated, this mattered little compared to the civilization Europe was bringing them. And when facts collided with myth, it was the facts that had to give way. Two notable cases are the lovely bronzes of Benin and Ife in Nigeria and the ruined city of Zimbabwe in Southern Rhodesia. Generations of European scholars groped far afield in the search for a non-African origin for artifacts and ruins that were proof of a relatively high level of art and technology. They were, various "experts" speculated, Portuguese, Arabic or perhaps Phoenician; they could not, according to the imperial myth, be African. The general opinion of today—that the Benin bronzes and Zimbabwe are indeed the work of black African civilizations—could not be accepted as long as the "primitive barbarism" of Africans was a major tenet of imperial belief.

The European belief in African "savagery" grew rather than diminished over the centuries of European influence in Africa. The reports of the Portuguese, the first Europeans in Africa, are strikingly different in tone from those of the nineteenth and twentieth centuries. "The early Portuguese, one may remark, had no contempt for these African states they found and traded with," Basil Davidson writes in *Old Africa Rediscovered*. Davidson attributes the growth of the myth of "natural African inferiority" to the decline of Africa under the impact of the slave trade and the corresponding advance of European technology.

The slave trade itself produced a vast spate of hypocrisy when Europeans tried to reconcile the human degradation of the trade with principles to which they at least paid lip service. Comments in Europe on the slave trade are often in vivid contrast to the blunt attitude of ancient Romans that a slave was simply an *instrumentum vocale,* a tool to be used as its owner saw fit without the intrusion of any moral questions. One common European view was that Africans do not feel pain as much as white people do; so whipping an African was not as reprehensible as whipping a white. In any case, slavery was a positive benefit, for the Africans were thus brought into the sphere of Christianity. It may also be that the imperial myth became increasingly necessary as Europe itself became democratic. In the sixteenth century, for an authoritarian state to hold colonies required little apology. But in the twentieth century, if Europeans could vote, why not Africans? The "natural inferiority" of Africans, their "innate racial inability to govern themselves properly," provided a convenient answer. One step further and imperial conquest, like slavery, became a favor to the conquered: Kipling's "white man's burden."

These attitudes have not entirely disappeared. That overworked cliché, the analogy between the European-African relationship and Prospero and Caliban in *The Tempest,* still crops up in writings on Africa. It takes, of course, an awesome degree of egocentricity, or ethnocentricity, to identify one's self or culture with Prospero: how smug it makes us feel! Nor is the analogy, as used, always true to its original, let alone to reality. In *Prospero and Caliban: The Psychology of Colonization,* O. Mannoni argued that Prospero is as psychologically dependent on Caliban as Caliban on Prospero; the

European master needs a servant to dominate as much as the African servant needs a master to dominate him. But Mrs. Elspeth Huxley, writing in 1964, only mentions African Caliban's dependence, not European Prospero's.

The European rulers of Africa, then, created a feudal society far different from the European societies from which they came. The gap between European and African was unbridgeable, with extremely rare exceptions. Whatever their individual talents, the white man commanded, the black man obeyed, for their positions were based on birth, not ability. The pomp and circumstance of European rule in the tropics, contrasting so strangely with the prosaic life of Europe itself, were outward symbols of the feudal right of the Europeans to rule: they were designed to "impress the natives." So the individual European put on his feudal mask. Whatever he did at home, in Africa he never worked with his hands. He lived in ostentatious splendor; his wife, who used to do the dishes in Manchester or Marseilles, had half a dozen servants about whom she complained incessantly. Little wonder that, despite their complaints, the Europeans were reluctant to go home and, when they did, often found themselves out of place in their own society; talk to an ex-colonial and you soon see how he misses the easy life and easier status of Africa. Not, it should be emphasized, that European rule in Africa was particularly brutal. Quite the contrary: colonial rule, in the twentieth century, at least, was probably as mild as any in the history of imperialism. What matters in the legacy that colonialism left to independent Africa is that the Africans saw a society in which power was based on birth, on color, on education, much more than on personal productivity. That was colonial-European culture, and in it God was unmistakably white.

Though generally mild, European rule was far from democratic. Ex-colonials often say that "we introduced the Africans to democracy," then go on to deplore the lack of democracy in independent Africa. It would be fairer to say—though a great exaggeration—that the Europeans introduced much of Africa to absolutism. For almost its entire course, European rule was an alien bureaucratic dictatorship resting ultimately on military force and in no way responsible to the people it governed. In the last years, the colonial powers introduced elections and some trappings of democracy, but the ultimate right of self-determination was withheld till the day independence was granted (except in the case of the 1958 de Gaulle referendum in the then French colonies). Bureaucratic dictatorship was the main colonial legacy. In most places in Africa, it was undoubtedly less responsible to the governed than was the African political system it replaced. African forms of government varied widely, but many, perhaps most, of them were relatively egalitarian, and the rulers' power was far from absolute. Two-way communications, in which the rulers listened to those they ruled as well as issuing orders, were certainly greater before than during the colonial period. Given the assumption of natural African inferiority, there could hardly be any reason for the colonials to consult the people before setting government policy. The white man knew best.

The colonial empires were not run entirely by Europeans. To run an empire more cheaply, and therefore more profitably, the Europeans used Africans in the lower levels of the administration as instruments of their rule. Similarly, the French settlers in eighteenth-century Haiti used mulattoes to oversee their African slaves. In Africa, it was obviously cheaper to use African employees rather than high-priced Europeans, provided the Africans were kept on the lower levels where they would not command Europeans. (In wartime, of course, Africans were used as cannon fodder on the battlefields of Europe.) In parts of Africa the British harnessed the existing chiefs to administer for them and save on British personnel; this system, known as "indirect rule," was put to its fullest use in northern Nigeria. The French did the same to some extent—they had an *école des fils de chef* at Dakar in the nineteenth century—but they depended increasingly on a "Europeanized" elite. For jobs as clerks and primary school teachers, literate Africans were needed. To produce this small "elite," the colonial authorities set up, or allowed missionaries to set up, a school system for Africans. Many of those who created and ran these schools had generous motives and wanted to educate Africans for the sake of education; but the reason the schools had to exist, their inner purpose, was to produce men to help operate the empire at lower cost. It is this class of African auxiliaries, educated in European-run schools, that has produced most of the present leaders of independent Africa. Dia of Senegal, Keita of Mali, Maga of Dahomey, Nkrumah of Ghana were school teachers; Touré of Guinea, Azikwe of Nigeria were clerks; Houphouet-Boigny of the Ivory Coast was a medical assistant.

The European school was usually the first contact today's African ruler had with the world outside his own society. The shock was often brutal. Like the colonial administration, the school taught the crushing superiority of all things European. Africa was not only inferior; it was almost nonexistent in the curriculum. The flora and fauna the African children studied were those of Europe; they followed the adventures of European children in a world they had never seen; if they went on to secondary education, they studied the history and literature of Britain and France. In the French colonies, black children recited the textbook that begins with the famous line: *"Nos ancêtres les gaulois . . ."* The African children's own ancestors were never mentioned, for they had, according to the myth, "no history." But if the child adopted the Gauls as his spiritual ancestors, he could become "evolved," a sort of black European. A synthetic product, of course, easily distinguished from the real thing; but in the imperial myth an imitation European was better than a real African. To prove that he had adopted this mock-European ancestry, the young African simply had to pass his school examinations, and for this memorization and obedience were more important than intelligence and imagination. Then he was entitled to a balcony seat in the colonial theater.

After graduation, the young Africans usually went into the service of their rulers. Typically they became clerks or teachers in primary schools. Now they were far above their uneducated fellows in status and privilege; but still of course far below the Europeans. Africans were discouraged from advancing past the inferior ranks of the administration. Even if "evolved," they were still essentially auxiliaries; it was hard, next to impossible, to reach a position of command. For to allow an African to command a European would have contradicted the essence of the colonial myth that Africans were incapable of ruling themselves. (The definition of "European" was not strictly racial. France used West Indians, many of them black, as administrators; Félix Eboué, a colonial governor during World War II, was a West Indian. But the West Indians were considered, and considered themselves, European.)

Among the African auxiliaries, prestige went to those in government jobs; rank within the government, and therefore on the prestige ladder, was determined primarily by the diploma one held. The Lebret study, a massive examination of Senegal on the eve of independence, said: "Within the civil servant class, the social and professional hierarchy is based on the hierarchy of apparent [European] culture. . . . The occupation that has the most prestige in the eyes of Senegalese, as soon as they have a minimum of education, is that of civil servant . . . for the majority of parents, education is equivalent to getting into public service, rather than to an improvement in ability to use techniques, as is the case in nations like the U.S.S.R. and the U.S.A." Here again the school reflected the values of the feudal colonial society, in which status was more important than ability or productivity. In both school and job, a creative personality was discouraged.

During his working life, the African government employee had to make his way in a system run on alien values, in which he was considered at best a necessary evil. African auxiliaries might be useful for economic reasons; they were hardly welcomed with open arms, and there were always Europeans around to remind the Africans overtly or by implication of their innate and unchangeable inferiority. In his private life, the African official still lived according to African culture. Symbolically, it was, and still is, common for African men to wear a European suit to go to work in the European world; then, when they are back in their African home, to change to long African robes. The educated African had to reconcile the African ways of his family with the often-conflicting demands made on him by his European masters. In many cases the result was a serious distortion of the African's personality. Joyce Cary, in *Mister Johnson,* describes from a European viewpoint the torment of an African clerk in Nigeria who destroys himself in the impossible attempt to satisfy the demands of two cultures. The conflict of cultures is the subject of most contemporary African literature. As a sort of counterpoint to Cary, the Nigerian novelist Chinua Achebe describes, this time from the African perspective, the destruction of a young educated Nigerian who, like Mister Johnson, is caught between the conflicting demands of Africa and Europe. In French-speaking Africa, the same theme occurs in *L'Aventure Ambigue,* an autobiographical novel by the Senegalese Sheikh Hamidou Kane, in which the protagonist loses first his soul and at last his life in the collision between Paris and his aristocratic Muslim background.

When they reminisce on their lives under European rule, many educated Africans show a lively awareness of the heavy psychological price in alienation and self-contempt that they paid for their privileged status as assistants to their foreign rulers. President Sékou Touré of Guinea has been, in political terms, the most anti-French of African leaders. Yet in 1959, a year after he defied de Gaulle and led his nation to independence, Touré said: "I find myself more at home with French friends than with my own elder brother who has never been to school. . . . Colonization meant that opportunities of advancement were open to a small African elite, but the cost was the creation of deep divisions between us." Outwardly Sékou Touré is a confident and extraordinarily magnetic man; these honest words give some indication of the inner turmoil he has suffered. Similarly, the Senegalese official Ibrahima Sow said, in a conversation about the past: "We lived withdrawn into ourselves. The deliberate orientation of our minds created complexes in us, and led us to passivity, opportunism and complicity with the [European] occupant." And Kwame Nkrumah, President of Ghana, wrote in bitter memory of the scars inflicted on him: "We were trained to be inferior copies of Englishmen, caricatures to be laughed at with our pretensions to British bourgeois gentility, our grammatical faultiness and distorted standards betraying us at every turn. We were neither fish nor fowl."

But the school the Europeans built to produce African auxiliaries helped to undermine their rule. "The first colonialist school killed colonialism," an African teacher, Samuel Doamba, wrote (with vast exaggeration). Inevitably, literate Africans came in contact with Europe, either through books or by study in Britain or France. They then saw the contradiction between European democracy and colonial feudalism. From Europe, Africans adopted such tools of protest as political parties and labor unions; often they picked up ideology from European leftists who were also, though for different reasons, in opposition to their governments. Educated Africans then hurled back at their rulers the democratic principles practiced in Europe but denied to Africa. It was they, the educated African auxiliaries, rather than the African masses, who began to agitate against colonial rule after the Second World War. Also among the agitators were ex-soldiers who had survived the European wars for which they were recruited.

The retreat of empire proved to be rapid and painless in Black Africa, except where there were large numbers of white settlers. The climate of opinion had turned against colonialism, the African colonies had never been very profitable or important, at least to Britain and

France; so, when their auxiliaries turned against them, they quickly withdrew from what had become a liability. Ghana became independent in 1957; in 1965 the great majority of black Africans are living under African rule. And when the Europeans left, they handed over power to those African ex-auxiliaries whom they had educated and who had learned to rule their fellow Africans in the colonial system.

When Africa became independent, the new rulers inherited economies that had been shaped according to the needs of Europe. To make the colonies pay, they had to produce something of value to Europe. The first cash crop that Africa supplied to Europe, and by far the most profitable, was human beings. From the sixteenth to the nineteenth centuries, Europe mined the human resources of Africa, though the Europeans did not yet govern the continent. The horrors of the transatlantic slave trade have been amply described; the effects of the trade on the interior of Africa, the ripping of its social fabric, can only be guessed at. Domestic slavery had existed before the Europeans came, but it was the introduction of cash value for large numbers of slaves that caused a profound upheaval in the African interior, where once peaceful tribes went to war to capture slaves for sale to the Europeans, fracturing society and setting each village against its neighbor. (The introduction of other cash crops later was to have a similar, though much milder, upsetting effect on Africa.) "Angola was a mere shambles, in which the criminal classes of Portugal were employed in inciting the native peoples to make war on each other in the interests of slave labour for Brazil," Oliver and Fage wrote in *A Short History of Africa.* Little is known about that time, but it is tempting to speculate that the nature of African village society is at least partly due to the atmosphere of fear and insecurity that reigned during the centuries of the slave trade.

After the slave trade died out in the nineteenth century, the Europeans cast about for other ways to make Africa profitable. In the late nineteenth and early twentieth centuries, they had extended their rule over almost the whole continent: this increased the operating cost of the European presence in Africa. Extraction, of one form or another, usually was the easiest and surest way to make money on a colony, and where minerals existed, mining was the most profitable form of extraction. In South Africa, the Europeans found gold and diamonds, and copper in the Rhodesias and Katanga. In South Africa, the Rhodesias and Kenya, the Europeans found a temperate winterless climate and fertile soil, so white settlers came to farm with cheap African labor. (Anyone who has seen how the settlers lived can understand their reluctance to go back to a homeland that is grim and cold by comparison.) West Africa, however, had relatively little to offer Europe after the slave trade. Minerals were few, other than some gold in Ghana (its name in colonial times was the Gold Coast) and diamonds in Sierra Leone. Bauxite and iron ore exist in a belt stretching through Guinea to Ghana, but their exploitation is recent. The generally poor soils, harsh climate and disease of West Africa, the "white man's grave," discouraged European settlement, thereby sparing that region bitter racial conflict. The nationalist party of Eastern Nigeria, the National Convention of Nigerian Citizens, adopted the malaria-carrying anopheles mosquito as its party symbol in ironic tribute to the insect for keeping white settlers away.

The European profit in West Africa was never as great as the Europeans once hoped and as many Africans still believe. The main effort of the Europeans was in trade. If the Africans were to pay taxes to support the European government, and if they were to buy European goods, they had to have money incomes. The Europeans took their taxes in the early days in the form of forced labor, but the imposition of money taxes had two effects useful to the colonial economy: it forced the Africans to grow cash crops or to go to work for white settlers. If trade was to flourish, there had to be improved lines of communication. This was the setting of colonial economic policy in West Africa.

African money income came from those cash crops that were useful to Europe. The five major crops were peanuts and oil palms (both responding to a growing European demand for vegetable oils), coffee, cacao and cotton. Ghana became the world's largest producer of cacao; Nigeria and the Congo produced oil palms for Unilever's soap; the Ivory Coast grew coffee and cacao; Guinea raised bananas and, later, pineapples; Senegal specialized in peanuts.

The change in Senegal, to take one example, from trade in human beings to trade in a cash crop may be dated from a symbolic incident that took place in 1840 in Dakar, whose offshore island, Gorée, was once a major depot for the slave ships. In that year an African chief approached a French chemist named Rousseau with some slaves for sale. Rousseau rejected that social contract but offered another kind of deal. "Keep your captives," he said to the chief, "but for peanuts I will give you anything you want from Europe." The chief decided it was more profitable to put his slaves to work growing peanuts than to sell them. The next day, according to a contemporary account, "the marabouts [Muslim leaders] were gathered together; they buried *gris-gris*

25

[charms] and promised to propagate the growing of peanuts." By the late nineteenth century peanuts made up half Senegal's exports; today the figure is 80 per cent and half the cultivated land in the nation is planted to peanuts. The peanuts were and are grown by African families on small plots; large-scale slavery died out in the late nineteenth century, and attempts to start mechanized plantations under European management were failures. The most economical way to manage the trade in peanuts, as in most other West African cash crops, was to stimulate the Africans to grow them by their need for cash to pay taxes and buy the goods the European traders were bringing into the bush.

Though the French in Senegal—and other Europeans elsewhere—did not make money on the actual growing of peanuts, they made a profit on the many other steps of the process that brought a bottle of oil to a French housewife's shelf and, at the other end, a European product to an African hut. The nature of the colonial economic system, which the French call *le pacte colonial,* was stated with a memorable bluntness in 1899 by Jules Meline, France's Minister of Agriculture. France should, Meline said, "discourage in advance those attempts at industrialization that may take place one day in our colonies; in a word, oblige our overseas possessions to address themselves exclusively to the metropole [France] for manufactured goods, and to fulfill—voluntarily or by force—their natural role as markets, reserved by privilege for metropolitan industry." Since the Europeans were in the saddle, they bought cheap and sold dear in a trading system rigged against the Africans.

Trade was controlled by a few large all-purpose companies that bought African produce and sold European goods in return. Two of the largest were—and are today

—the British-Dutch Unilever trust and the French Compagnie Française de l'Afrique Occidentale. Unilever started oil palm plantations in the then Belgian Congo. It buys African-grown palm oil in Nigeria, and operates under various names in the French colonies: in the Ivory Coast Unilever appears under the odd disguise of Compagnie Française de la Côte d'Ivoire. There was little competition and much interlocking control among the colonial trading companies, as René Gendarme showed, in the case of Madagascar, in *L'Economie de Madagascar*. Just as the political rulers of Africa instituted a sort of feudal system that no longer existed in Europe, so the trading companies practiced the economics of scarcity that was disappearing from the European commercial system. Trade did not lead in most cases to increased African productivity and wealth. High markups, low volume, inefficient transportation and distribution—all combined to raise the price of goods that entered the trading system. (The fish that sells for 10¢ on the dock at Tamatave in Madagascar costs $1 in Tananarive, 230 miles by train on the railroad that is said to have the highest freight rates in the world.) The voteless African consumer was much more at the mercy of the trading company than was a European consumer: the result was that the African, who earned much less than a European, paid more for goods that were inferior. The junk that Europe sold to Africa was in the tradition of the legendary purchase of Manhattan for beads, or the signing away by African chiefs of huge tracts of land in return for a few baubles. The agronomist René Dumont tells of trying to buy an alarm clock from a Greek trader in the Congo. The trader refused to sell Dumont the clock. "It's a trade clock. It will only run for a few days," the trader explained. Much the same happened to us in Guinea, with the difference that in our case the trader did not refuse to sell the clock and did not explain that it would fail in a short time. It did.

When African peasants gave up their old subsistence crops in favor of the new cash crop, they were in effect putting themselves in the hands of the traders, from whom they were now forced to buy such necessities as clothing and even food. The traders were not slow to exploit their advantage. By usury and such forms of cheating as rigged scales, the trader could recoup a large part of the theoretical price that he paid for the Africans' crops. When the peasant sold his crop, he was encouraged to spend his cash on baubles or overpriced imported cloth. Then, before his next crop, he would run out of food, since he no longer produced enough to feed his family. The trader would advance him food at rates of interest of up to 100 per cent for six months. When the peasant brought in his crop, the trader would deduct the interest, and often shortweigh the crop in the bargain. Once involved in the cycle of usury, it was next to impossible for the peasant to escape—he was at the mercy of the trader. According to one estimate, the Senegalese peanut grower actually realized about half of the posted price at which his crop was bought.

Since he had neither economic nor political bargaining power, the terms of trade—the goods he received for the crops he sold—tended to turn against the African producer. From 1913 to 1930 the price of Senegalese peanuts multiplied by 3.5, but the price of imported cloth (the peasants' main purchase) rose by 7.7 times. In 1936 the peasant who sold 100 kilos of peanuts could buy more than 100 kilos of rice with the proceeds; today it takes 145 kilos of peanuts to buy 100 kilos of rice. These are examples of a longterm trend in trade relations between the industrial nations of the north and the tropical south; for the past century or more, the trend has been against the south, with a few exceptions caused mostly by wars. The trading companies could work out three-cornered deals with other colonies. At one time, rice from French Indo-China was sold at .55 franc *retail* in France—and at 1.00 franc *wholesale* in Africa. It was to the companies' benefit when the Africans no longer grew all their own food, for it increased their dependence on the trader; in the same way, the traders actively discouraged African handicrafts and artisanry. The result was a decline in the technological level of many villages; people who once made their clothing and tools now bought imports.

The introduction of the money economy, as conceived in colonial days, had fateful consequences for Africa that linger on after the end of colonial rule. Because the import-export trade was favored over internal trade, the lines of communication built by the Europeans stretch from the inland producing districts to the port from which goods will be shipped to Europe. In most African countries, there are few roads or railroads serving the nation's internal trade, and that trade therefore is stifled in favor of imports. The details are sometimes ludicrous. In Cotonou, capital of Dahomey, a man who heard we were leaving by road for Lagos, capital of Nigeria, asked us to mail a letter for him in Lagos. It is less than a day's drive from Cotonou to Lagos, but his letter would have gone by air to Paris, from there to London, from London to Lagos.

Colonial rule is often praised for stimulating the growth of cash crops, and there is no doubt that production for export has greatly increased. But whether there has been a corresponding increase in Africa's produc-

29

tivity or wealth is questionable. Most of the increase has been achieved not by increasing per-acre production, but by planting more acres. With few exceptions, the new crops are grown with methods that are at least as destructive to the soil as traditional African agriculture. More production, of course, means more destruction of soil. In this sense, much cash crop agriculture is extraction, the mining of agricultural capital, under the stimulus of the European-introduced money economy, just as in the slave trade Africans mined their human resources in response to European demand. Nor have the Africans got much in return for the sale of their land's fertility; on balance, it is likely that more rural Africans have suffered than benefited from switching to cash crops. Their money income has obviously risen, but their standard of living has probably fallen. Their diet, especially, was probably poorer in 1960 than in 1860, because they were no longer able to grow all their own food. This has been argued in the case of the cacao farmers of Ghana, and if it is true of them, the most prosperous farmers of West Africa, it was almost certainly true of others who made the change.

Among nations, as among men, trade between the strong and the weak is hardly likely to benefit the weak. In the words of Gunnar Myrdal, "a quite normal result of unhampered trade between two countries, of which one is industrialized and the other less developed, is the initiation of a cumulative process towards the impoverishment and stagnation of the latter." For the future, the most important consequence of colonialism will be that Africa was economically tied to the wheels of Europe. Before the Europeans came, African farmers were self-sufficient at an extremely low level. By the time the Europeans left, Africa had become what they

wanted: an economic appendage of Europe, with no
rational economy of its own, dependent on Europe for
all its manufactured goods, much of its clothing, even
some of its food, and selling its crops in European-con-
trolled markets. Less than 10 per cent of the new African nations' foreign trade is with each other; the rest
goes overseas. A stroke of the pen was, in some cases, all
that was needed to give Africa political freedom, but
far more is needed, as we shall see in later chapters, to
win for Africa the economic independence that would
bring about true freedom.

CHAPTER THREE

Stability and Stress
in Rural Africa

FROM WHATEVER PERSPECTIVE the traveler looks at rural Africa, he can see the distinctive patterns of man's relationship to the land and to other men. Flying over the tropics, he sees not the familiar rectangular farms of the West, but a series of circles scalloped out of the green forest; one clearing is now being farmed, another was recently abandoned and is half overgrown, still another has completely reverted to forest but its outline, like a faint scar, is still distinguishable. Walking around African farmland, the visitor would find it hard to tell who owns what and what is crop and what bush. No lines mark the boundaries of the farm, and he sees no straight planted rows; different crops are jumbled together in an anarchy that is, however, only apparent. In an African village, the homes are not arranged in quadrangles of single-family units, squares within the squares formed by streets meeting neatly at 90-degree angles. The huts usually are round, and grouped within a compound that is roughly circular. Everything seems shifting rather than permanent: the farms move every few seasons, and none of the huts are more than a few years old. He is, the perceptive Westerner will realize, in a world whose shape is different from that of his own world: a world of curves and circles, not straight lines and rectangles; of shifting relationships rather than fixed points.

This unfamiliar geometry symbolizes the adaptation man has made to the African environment. Almost any facet of African life—from land tenure to politics—is best understood in terms of circles and interrelationships; African philosophies deal far more in relatives than in absolutes. A new perspective, then, is the first essential step toward seeing the shape of rural Africa.

The land itself imposes these patterns. The soil from which Africans live is generally poor. Neither the semiarid savanna nor the tropical rain forest makes rich farmland, and the meager fertility of African soils is easily destroyed. In the savanna, the land is baked during the long dry season, and when it rains, the rainfall is too heavy and too short for the land to take full advantage of the water it receives. Despite its luxuriant growth of trees, the soil of the rain forest provides poor nourishment for food crops. Almost nowhere in Africa is it possible to keep land under continuous cultivation.

Over the centuries Africans have worked out ways of extracting a living from this harsh land. They farm by what is called "shifting cultivation" or "bush fallow." The land is cleared by the destructive practice of setting fire to the cover: though some fertility is added to the soil, much of it goes up in smoke. The cleared land is planted for one to three seasons; then it is abandoned for as much as twenty years to revert to bush and slowly regain its exhausted fertility. When he prepares his land, the African farmer barely scratches the soil with his hoe, and he does not clear all the trees and roots. He mixes his crops: yams underground, for example, with several kinds of vegetables planted over them. In these methods, the Africans are following sound agricultural principles on which it is, at least at present, difficult to improve. By not clearing any more than necessary, he disturbs the soil as little as possible, reducing the possibility of wind and water erosion and other forms of damage. By mixing his crops without straight rows, he imitates the way plants grow naturally; it is characteristic of the tropics that many kinds of plants grow together in bewildering confusion. He cannot master his environment, so the African farmer adapts to it.

But the equilibrium between man and the land provides only a bare and difficult living. Since each acre in production requires at least five acres in fallow, the land cannot support many people, and every couple of years the farmer must go through the arduous job of clearing still another piece of bush. The returns are meager; few farmers get as little food for their effort as the Africans. Neither animal power nor the wheel are used to supplement man's muscle, and the only tools available to most African farmers are a short-handled hoe (the *daba*) and a knife; their equipment is, in the words of L.-J. Lebret, "more primitive than that of ancient Egypt." (Lebret's statement may come as a shock to those of us in whom the belief in the inevitability of progress is inbred, but it applies to a large part of the globe today.)

The African peasant, especially the man, is frequently called "indolent." He is indeed idle during part of the year, but all nature conspires against him. His heavy labor, from planting to harvesting, comes at the worst time of the year: the rainy season, when the air is op-

pressively hot and humid and his reserves of food from
the last crop are running low. The little return he gets
for his painful effort hardly encourages him to work
beyond the needs of sheer survival. If African men are
often underemployed, the women are not, for the divi-
sion of labor between them is far from even. The men
eat before the women, and they take the best morsels,
but it is women who do most of the work in Africa. In
a typical village scene, the men are chatting or sleeping
under a tree, while the women are grinding the family's
food in a mortar, endlessly lifting and dropping the
heavy wooden pestle. While African men work from 60
to 80 days a year in the rain forest, and 100 to 150 in the
savanna, according to René Dumont, "the majority of
African farm women are fully employed, and many are
overworked." Dumont gives examples of societies where
the women do most of the farm work plus all the domestic duties. The men do the heavy labor of clearing the
fields, but usually it is the woman who cares for the
growing crop. Her domestic work is long. The woman is
responsible for gathering wood and bringing water to
the home. She has no mechanical or animal help: no
donkey to carry the wood and water, no cart; not even
a pulley at the well. She must carry it all on her head;
the African woman pays a heavy price for her beautiful
erect posture. In the savanna country, where wood is
sparse and wells are few, a woman may spend up to six
hours a day on these two tasks alone. In addition, she
works in the fields, grinds and cooks the food, and cares
for her many children.

All through their lives, Africans are attacked by an
impressive number of natural enemies; sickness, not
health, is the norm of their existence. European medicine has reduced the great killing diseases—yellow fever,

smallpox, plague—and has made a start on sleeping sickness and leprosy. But there remains a host of ailments that sap a man's strength without killing him, at least not immediately, diseases that leave him diminished for all the years till he dies. The streets of many African cities are crowded with the crippled, the blind, the lepers; there are villages in West Africa and the Sudan where the entire adult population is blind. Most Africans suffer from not one but several chronic and debilitating ailments. The list is depressingly long: malaria, responsible for one-third of the death rate and chronic among millions; sleeping sickness; bilharzia, caused by a fresh-water mollusk that crawls through the skin and into the blood stream and eventually affects the organs; worm diseases like filariasis and hookworm; and the many forms of dysentery.

Many of these diseases tend to reduce the effective diet of Africans, for they prevent the absorption of food by the body. Even without parasites, the diet is inadequate. Africans usually get enough to eat—unlike some Asians—or at least enough to fill their bellies, though there is often a "hungry season" before the harvest. But their diet is lacking in proteins, especially animal proteins, and vitamins. (In many parts of Africa, the tse-tse fly makes it impossible to keep cattle.) The protein deficiency from which most Africans suffer diminishes both physical and mental stamina. In its most visible form, protein deficiency results in kwashiorkor, the disease that afflicts a child newly weaned from milk to starches that contain little protein. These children, their bellies swollen and hair turned reddish, are a common sight, particularly in West Africa. Many die of kwashiorkor, and the survivors are often stunted in their growth. But many Africans who never show the outward symptoms of kwashiorkor suffer from the effects of protein deficiency. The results have often been observed by teachers who have African and European children in the same class. At the beginning of the school day, both Africans and Europeans do their lessons, or run around the yard, with about the same amount of energy. But after a couple of hours the African children begin to droop, their strength drained, while the Europeans go on with undiminished vigor. The African children—who may, in addition to their chronic shortage of protein, have gone to school on an empty stomach—now seem passive and uninterested in what is going on around them. Their intelligence is not necessarily impaired; but their ability to use it is. Among African adults, protein deficiency may help account for what appears to be apathy and lack of initiative. And, of course, the many ailments which afflict Africans feed each other: one sickness leaves the body less able to defend itself against another.

In this hostile and unrewarding environment, malnourished and sapped by disease, Africans turn for support to the group. Alone, man is helpless; together, men can at least come to terms with nature. Much more than in Western societies, a rural African's prime concern is his relationship to the groups to which he belongs. The rules governing those relations and man's relation to the land he farms are the distinctive fabric of African rural society. The basic unit of living, as reflected in village housing, is larger in Africa than in Europe. The African unit is a compound that may contain fifty or even a hundred people. Within it are separate dwellings, but the fence—the line that divides one group from the next —surrounds the entire compound, not the units within it. The compound is inhabited by an "extended family." At its center is usually the hut of the patriarch, the oldest man, who is the family head. Around it are grouped the huts of his wives and their married children and perhaps other relatives. Although the milling crowds of children and chickens give an impression of chaos, life in the compound is conducted according to precise rules that leave little latitude to the individual. For anyone within the compound, his relationship to another individual—even by marriage—is less important than his position within the extended family.

The extended family is one of several concentric circles within which the African individual lives. He also belongs to his clan (a larger family unit), the village community, his tribe (an unsatisfactory word, but I know of no substitute; "ethnic group" is too ugly). Each of these groups is defined by kinship. The members of the village community usually are (or believe themselves to be) descended from a single First Ancestor, the semimythical person who founded the village. The individual finds his place in the world around him according to his ancestry, not according to any accomplishment of his own. Members of each circle owe each other specific obligations, diminishing as the circles get larger; the way men treat each other is determined not by abstract principles nor even by friendship, but by their degree of blood relation. A "good" man, in this society, is a man who fulfills all his obligations to the kinship circles to which he belongs. Harmony with the other members of the group, not diligence or accomplishment, is the path to acceptance and happiness. Security lies in the group, and the individual who belongs to no group is an outlaw, for he has no place in a world determined by kinship.

The hierarchy of groups, from family to tribe, dominates its members throughout their lives, and in the

hereafter. Its values are handed down by education. As
in any culture, education goes on constantly, but its most
important phase is the initiation that takes place during
adolescence. Boys and girls are taken from their homes
to a place some distance away where they are put in the
hands of the village priests and priestesses. Here they are
indoctrinated in the rules of the community, rules but-
tressed by the magic of religion. They are taught, often
with great harshness, how an adult works and behaves.
Those rules are laid down in the name of the First Ancestor, whose position is something like that of Moses.
Like Moses, the First Ancestor brought the people of the
village to their land, and, again like Moses, he laid down
a code, sanctified by religion, that regulates village life
(for example, methods of farming) in great detail. The
treatment of the boys and girls during initiation may be
cruel, but it is not purposeless: the individual is literally
beaten into the mold of the community. The young people who went out as boys and girls come back as men and
women; they may even take new names to symbolize
their entry into the adult world. The lifelong bond of
the age-grade—still another circle enclosing the individual—was described by the African author Birago
Diop:

> The brotherhood which begins in the initiation hut
> is stronger than brotherly love, more tyrannical
> than fatherly love; it subordinates the man worthy
> of his condition to certain rules, certain obligations,
> to certain laws that he cannot transgress without
> being lowered in the eyes of all others. Having
> mixed the blood of your sex at the age of twelve
> with the blood of another boy, lying on the ground
> in the cool daybreak; having sung with him the

39

same initiatory songs, having received the same blows and eaten with him the same good or stinking foods in the same calabashes; having grown to manhood at the same time, in the same hut . . . all this makes you the slave of his wishes, the servant of his wants, the captive of his worries.

In this world, the line between the living and the dead becomes blurred, for if the group is immortal and the individual is an organic part of the group, then he too has a measure of immortality. In parts of South and East Africa, a man who dies childless will be posthumously married. The children of his "wife," whose biological father may be the dead man's brother, are accepted as the children of the dead husband—thus he is assured a place in the endless line that links the dead through the living to the generations to come. In Madagascar, the dead are placed in a tomb above the ground. Whenever the family can afford it, the bones of their ancestors are brought out and wrapped in new cloth and paraded around the compound. It is a festive occasion, for the family is showing the ancestors what has happened since they went away. To many Westerners, this custom seems silly or disgusting; still worse, it is *uneconomic,* since the family spends a great deal on cloth and feasting. But to the Malagasies, it demonstrates the continuing membership of the dead in the immortal society of the group.

Similarly, land rights in Africa are generally held by the group, living and dead, rather than the individual. In the phrase of a Nigerian chief: "I conceive that land belongs to a vast family of which many are dead, few are living, and countless members are still unborn." Land tenure varies, but ownership along Western lines is virtually unknown in Africa. Here as elsewhere, law

follows the principles of society, and those who do not
grasp the nature of African traditional society are inevitably baffled when they ask who "owns" the land. The
land "belongs" to a community that stretches back to
the First Ancestor. The community's right to its land is
less a legal title than a biological relationship, a marriage
between the productive forces of man and the soil; the
soil is often described as a woman made fertile by the
action of man. The basic right to the land belongs to the
man who first cleared it and his descendants; each member of the group has the right to farm enough land to
support himself. This is a right to use land, not ownership of any particular acreage. Kinship, not geography,
is what matters. Within the community, families may
have rights over the land they farm, and couples within
the extended family may have their own plots. But their
rights derive only from their membership in the community. In some African societies, land may be sold, but
only to another member of the community or the clan
—another descendant, therefore, of a common ancestor.
If, as sometimes happens, land is sold to an outsider, it
is usually because he has become a member of the community. The transaction is not primarily commercial:
the person gets the land as a consequence of his adoption into the community.

The land, then, is inalienable, inseparable from the
community (unless the people move away). Even conquest does not necessarily destroy the community's
rights. It was common in parts of Africa for a conqueror
foreign to the community to continue to pay religious
tribute to the local First Ancestor, in effect recognizing
his predominant right over the land. The Europeans of
course did not recognize any rights they could not understand. In the areas they wanted to settle, they seized

land or bought it from the chiefs. Under African law, these transactions were unlawful: how could anyone sell land to an outsider when it belonged to the dead and the unborn as well as the living? The result in the "White Highlands" of Kenya was a flat contradiction between the two systems of law: in Western law, the land a white settler bought belongs to him; in African law, it belongs to the Kikuyu community. As a practical matter, of course, such issues were settled by power rather than by law.

Land tenure in Africa reflects economic as well as social realities. Under the system of shifting cultivation, where land is abandoned for long stretches of time, land in itself has no real value. What gives it value is the work men do to clear and plant it. Usually, then, the land "belongs" to the family that cleared it as long as they continue to farm it; when they abandon it, the land lies idle until, its fertility restored, another family then invests the work needed to clear it and once more give it value. Different rights may exist on the same land, according to what has been planted. In eastern Guinea, for example, the family that plants a kola tree has a right to its fruits during the tree's life. That family may abandon the land itself, and another family in time may clear it again and plant crops. But the first family still owns the product of the kola tree. Since the amount of land a family can work is strictly limited by their numbers and their tools, there is little point in having any more land than they can handle. In some parts of Africa, where the population growth has made land scarce—eastern Nigeria and the Kikuyu areas of Kenya are examples—the old system is beginning to change. Land scarcity will impel Africans toward permanent rather than shifting cultivation. The ultimate legal forms of land tenure are, as we shall see later, a thorny social and economic problem.

The flavor of African traditional society, and the way it affects those who live in it, is not easily conveyed to Westerners. When the rigid pattern of African village life is described, Westerners are likely to think: "Ah, yes, conformity. Well, we have that problem too. Look at the housing developments! All those books written about what conformists we are!" Man is of course a tribal animal, and there are tensions in Western society between the rights of the individual and those of the community. But one seldom finds such tensions in African society (except where colonial influence was strong) for there is no cause for conflict: the individual is submerged in the community; his conformity is ingrained from the day of his birth.

The differences between the influences on Western and African man are profound. Two are fundamental: privacy and communications. Westerners spend a good deal of their time alone, free with their thoughts, away from other members of their tribal groups. The African villager is almost never alone. He sleeps in a hut with several other people; he works in the fields with others; he eats with others; he relaxes with others. He is always with other people—the same people—and if only by force of habit, that seems to be the way he wants it. Loneliness, in which the slight paranoia of the unconforming genius breeds, is not part of the villagers' lives. Furthermore, Westerners are constantly in communication with people and ideas that come from outside their little group: we read newspapers and books, we are exposed to television and radio; we work and travel and eat with people whose education or experience is to some degree different from our own. Compare this to the African in his village. He is illiterate, so he does not read (and if he did know how to read, there would be nothing relevant to his life for him to read). Months, perhaps years, may go by in which he has no communication with anyone outside his community. The people he spends his days with grew up in the same community, went through the same initiation; even the work they do is the same as his. Since there is no communication, the African villager's mind becomes closed to receiving ideas from the outside—it is not part of his way of life. He is not intolerant of outsiders; they are just irrelevant to him.

Village society tends to reject change, especially by individuals, as part of its inner nature. In the perspective of villagers, innovation will be seen as a positive evil. The First Ancestor found a way of surviving in their hostile environment; the survival of the community depends on obedience to the rules he laid down. When the existing methods of farming are enforced by religion, an effort to change them is something like advising a devout Muslim or Orthodox Jew to eat pork because it is nourishing. Disobedience to the rules—for whatever reason—is disloyalty to the community; and the individual's main motive is to stay in harmony with those around him. The innovating farmer of the American type seldom exists in African traditional society; indeed he virtually cannot exist there. African society does not encourage this sort of personality; if one pops up by accident, he is hardly likely to have the respect of his fellows. For an African villager, the economic gain of some new technique would be a poor compensation for his loss of security if he got out of step with his fellows. Probably the issue does not even come up in that form in the villager's mind. Conditioned by his rigid education and the monotonous life he leads, the villager is likely to dismiss a possible change as distasteful, without consciously weighing its advantages and disadvantages.

The conservatism of African village society obviously is a tremendous barrier to change of any kind, even change that may in a sense be desired by the villagers themselves; Africans, after all, do not *want* to be sick or hungry or poor. The African village blocked most of the efforts of the Europeans to make it change, and is still defeating the efforts of the independent African governments. Yet African villages have innovated in the past; they are not unalterably opposed to change. In their migrations across the continent, some of which were fairly recent, Africans have had to adapt their techniques to innumerable new conditions. Some new crops have been rapidly adopted in Africa. Cassava (manioc), introduced in the fifteenth century, is now a standard food, and the new cash crops brought by the Europeans have also spread rapidly. Why new ways are adopted or not adopted in rural Africa is far from being clearly understood, but it is obvious that Africans do not always reject all changes. There is some evidence that innovations rejected by individual villagers can be introduced through the village leadership. Speaking through village leaders, the First Ancestor or the gods may approve of the change, and therefore the social fabric is kept intact. The growing of peanuts in Senegal, mentioned in Chapter Two, was decided upon by chiefs and Muslim leaders, who performed a ceremony giving religious sanction to the new crop. A more recent example is from Madagascar. In traditional Malagasy culture, work is forbidden on many days set aside for the gods. These idle days, which may have had a function in the past, came to interfere with new opportunities for increased farm production. In one village not long ago, the priests consulted the gods and then informed the people that the gods wanted the idle days to be given up. Like Mr. Dooley's Supreme Court, the gods were following the election returns; they endorsed the desires of the village leadership, and so conflict between the old and the new was avoided.

The social structure of an African village, the context within which such changes are attempted, does not fit easily into Western terminology. The many collective activities in village life have led some to believe that European-style cooperatives could readily be introduced. But in many African societies the collective and the individual are mixed. It is common, for example, for production to be individual and consumption collective. What this means is that each individual in an extended family will farm his own plot; even a husband and his wives will not work the same land. But the crops they produce are then shared as needed among all members of the unit. "Communocratic" is the word used by Sékou Touré, president of Guinea, to describe the village political system. It is neither "democratic" nor "dictatorial" as we understand the terms. Since the community is supreme, no individual can be a tyrant. Every individual, even the chief, is limited in his powers by the rigid rules of the community, though no constitution may define those limits. (In many parts of East Africa, the community was governed by the elders, the heads of extended families; the institution of the chief was introduced by the Europeans.) African chiefs are often worshiped, and inevitably the observer thinks of Louis XIV, or perhaps Josef Stalin. But the chief is worshiped not for himself, but as the incarnation and symbol of the First Ancestor; the chief is the human vessel into which the community's magic is poured. If the vessel is unworthy, it is discarded. In most communities, the chieftaincy is not hereditary. The chief is chosen by the elders and they can unseat him if he proves unsatisfactory. Among the Ashanti of Ghana, the chief was "enstooled" in his office with these warnings:

Tell him that
We do not wish for greediness
We do not wish that he should curse us
We do not wish that his ears should be hard of
*   hearing*
We do not wish that he should call people fools
We do not wish that he should act on his own
*   initiative*
We do not wish things done as in Kumasi
We do not wish that it should ever be said: "I have
*   no time. I have no time."*
We do not wish personal abuse
We do not wish personal violence.

Hedged around with such prohibitions, the chief is less a dictator than a sort of ikon, a visual symbol of the community. When the Serers of Senegal went to war, they filled their chief's trousers with earth, immobilizing him on the battlefield like a flag; he lived or died according to the fortune of battle. The chief may be highly privileged, but those privileges are accorded to him as symbol, not as man, and do not represent any great power in his hands. In any case, the chief has also undergone the rigid training of initiation and is likely to want to conform to the community rules.

The chief presides over a community which is under obligation to keep each individual as a member, to make sure that no one suffers the fate of exile. The power of the community is limited by the need for the consent, not just of a majority, but of all or almost all its members. When you attend an African palaver, you see this obligation in action. The leaders and those who speak on public affairs—usually adult males above a certain age—are gathered together, under a tree or in a simple building. The palaver seems as if it will never end: it rambles on for hours or days. Everyone who wants to speak is heard, and what he says need not be relevant to the issue for which the palaver was held. More than once I have heard mild efforts by Europeanized Africans to hold discussion to the subject blocked by the general feeling that every man has the right to say what he wants. Earlier I mentioned the Westernized engineer who angrily silenced an irrelevant and abusive heckler and was rebuked himself. As in any African palaver, the harmony of the group mattered far more than reaching a majority decision or an effective course of action. Accordingly, voting is not part of the palaver; the talking simply goes on until everyone has had his say and a feeling of harmony prevails.

The village community is in many ways more egalitarian than most societies. The system of land tenure means that, in contrast to Asia and Latin America, there are no African landowners living off the labor of tenants or serfs. Since everyone does the same work on much the same amount of land, most of the families in the village have about the same income. Families of low caste or of slave ancestry are low in status, but not necessarily poorer than the rest; they are less subject to the whim of others than, say, an Indian peon on a hacienda in the Andes.

Westerners, and many educated Africans, believe that this traditional African culture must disappear as the small world of the village is opened to outside influences. Already the old culture is crumbling, and few villages

remain untouched by the forces of change. The impact
of Europe is continuing. Even what appear to be minor
changes tear the social fabric. Growing a cash crop, for
example, brings a village into the money economy, undermining the whole pattern of living. The transistor
radio now penetrates deep into the bush, blaring new
ideas. European-style education, that tool with which
the colonial rulers sliced a small minority of Africans
away from their fellows, is reaching greater numbers
every year. Yet traditional culture shows great vitality.
Even among the "Europeanized," even in the cities,
many traditional values persist, influencing the ways in
which Africans adapt to their new environment.

When traditional society does crumble under the impact of the West, the result is likely to be autocracy
rather than democracy. The rigid restraints that African
"communocracy" places on its leaders are loosened. The
satisfying security of the old way of life is destroyed, and
little is offered in its place. In this spiritual vacuum,
people may turn to the certainties offered by an absolutism unfettered by the outdated rules of the community. By undermining traditional society, Europe
may leave irresponsible forms of dictatorship as its
gloomy legacy to Africa. President Kwame Nkrumah of
Ghana has been criticized by Africans for taking on the
trappings of chieftaincy while refusing to accept the restraints which (as we saw in the example of the Ashanti)
bind the chief; in varying degree, this tendency exists in
most new African states.

The Murid sect that arose in Senegal half a century
ago is an extreme example of what dangerous growths
can take root in the ruins of traditional Africa. The sect
was founded by Amadou Bamba, a Muslim notable at
the court of Lat Dior, last of the precolonial kings of the

Wolofs of Western Senegal. The origin and rise of the Murid sect coincided with the French conquest, which seems to have had a particularly destructive effect on the Wolofs. Bamba's first converts were Wolof soldiers, fleeing after their defeat by the French. In the chaos and insecurity of the conquest, the Wolofs flocked to the new way of life offered by Amadou Bamba. When he died in 1927, the French were firmly in control of Senegal, but the members of the sect, who now number at least 500,000, belonged to Amadou Bamba.

Though Muslim in its theology, Muridism is a distinctive society. It is an extraordinary theocracy. Its leader, Falilou M'Backé, son of Amadou Bamba, combines in his person the powers of a medieval pope, Josef Stalin and a nineteenth-century factory owner. Like the pope, he is the single and unquestioned interpreter of the will of God to his people. Like Stalin, he administers their lives as he pleases and dictates their politics at election time. And, like the early industrialist, he exploits his people's labor to the limit of human capacity.

Body and soul, the Murid belongs to the M'Backé family and their appointed agents. For a promised reward in the next world, the Murid disciple gives all the goods of this world to his *marabout* (the West African word for a Muslim cleric). In the Murid regions, there are villages named M'Backé, after the ruling family, in which the people also use M'Backé as their family name. Since first names are limited here—half the men bear the name "Mamadou," the African version of Mohammed—there are hundreds of men named Mamadou M'Backé who live in M'Backé. In a literal way, they have abandoned their individual identities and merged themselves with the prophet who rules them.

The M'Backé family's exploitation of its followers is

ruthless. Early converts to the cash economy, they are
the great peanut growers of Senegal. Murid disciples
turn over all their crop to the marabout. He markets
their peanuts, and returns to them the bare minimum
necessary to sustain life. Since the Wolofs are not good
farmers—the neighboring Serers get 30 per cent more
peanuts to the acre—it would not seem that there was
much to be squeezed out of them; the French found it
impossible to grow peanuts profitably with plantation
labor, slave or free. But the voluntary slavery of Muridism is profitable indeed. In addition to the profits of the
peanut trade, the family collects an estimated $800,000
each August from the faithful who visit the tomb of
Amadou Bamba in the holy city of Touba. The Murid
leaders are wheeler-dealers in the early capitalist tradition. With soiled bills collected during the August pil-
grimage, they buy new Cadillacs every six months; they
speculate on the peanut market and were reported recently to be planning to build a chain of hotels. The
frank combination of religion and business is nicely sym-
bolized by a gas station, on the outskirts of Touba, that
bears this name: "Station Shell du Grand Marabout
Falilou M'Backé."

The grip of the M'Backés on the Murids is restrained
neither by Islam nor by the time-honored rules of village
society nor by European ideas of democracy and social
justice. The M'Backés make the rules. In theory the
Murid marabout teaches his disciples the Koran in return for their labor, but in practice this obligation is
increasingly disregarded, and the streets of Dakar swarm
with students sent out to beg by their marabouts. Such
a violation of principle might well cause the ouster of a
chief in traditional African society—not the Murid
marabout. "Follow your marabout as a dog follows its

master," Amadou Bamba told his disciples, and: "You must be like the donkey who does not eat the millet he is carrying." The Murids follow their masters, without a leash. No barbed wire surrounds the M'Backé kingdom to keep the people in; the family operates no concentration camps to punish opposition. The marabouts do not seem to fear the corrupting effects of the city; often they send young men to work in Dakar during the dry season, and the young men give their earnings to the marabout. Defections are rare. The Murid disciple who gives up everything for his marabout is apparently satisfied with the security he gets in return.

Muridism is by no means typical of Africa. Yet its origin in a typically African situation, the collapse of traditional society under European attack, makes it a disturbing illustration of what can happen in Africa. The willing submission of the Murids to the unbounded power of their leaders is, also, a tempting example to those who believe that dictatorship is the necessary road to modernization.

CHAPTER FOUR

The Elite in Power

ALL OF A SUDDEN, the Europeans were gone. What had happened was more *coup d'état* than revolution. Few rural Africans were involved in the political events leading to independence; no revolutionary wars had destroyed the structure of colonial and traditional society. Preindependence politics was in the hands of the urban Africans who were the auxiliaries of the ruling Europeans. When the Europeans abruptly left, they handed over the machinery of power to their ex-auxiliaries. The palaces were not burned, the jails were not destroyed; the offices and symbols of power were taken over, in their existing form, by the African elite. The future of Africa's rural majority would to a large degree depend on the elite's attitudes and the circumstances in which they took power.

The new rulers were men marked indelibly by the experience of European rule. If they hated their white masters, nonetheless they had absorbed from them many European colonial values, including something of the European contempt for Africans. If there was much about them that was African, yet they were alienated from traditional African society. By the circumstances of their coming to power, the African elites were faced with a profound contradiction. Painfully aware of the inequities of colonial rule, influenced by the European left, they took power impregnated with an ideology that called for social justice. Some preached reform and some revolution, but none reaction or plain conservatism; though it is vaguely defined, "African socialism," the slogan of most of the new rulers, reflects the wish for change, and, in many cases, a desire to restore some of the values of traditional African culture. But the facts of their coming to power were in vivid contrast to this ideology. The elite was in effect handed the control of a feudal society. When the Europeans surrendered the keys of the palace, they put the elite in their own shoes: alien masters of a world in which the gap between ruler and ruled was a chasm, and power and privilege were deliberately concentrated in that tiny alien minority. The people passively accepted alien rule, first by alien Europeans, then by alienated Africans. Nothing could be more natural than for the African elite to continue a system in which they were so highly privileged; social change would inevitably reduce their power, their income, their sense of superiority.

The record of the African elites in power has been shaped by this contradiction between ideology and circumstance. Two souls live in the African rulers' breasts, and their coexistence is uneasy. "Africa has no classes," say Leopold Senghor of Senegal and Sékou Touré of Guinea; yet both Presidents have shown that they are aware of the deep divisions within their people that make it more accurate to say, as Disraeli said of nineteenth-century Britain, that Africa is divided not into two classes, but into two races.

The elite's performance is shaped, also, by its own peculiar nature. The African ruling class is notably different from the ruling class of many underdeveloped nations. Because of the nature of African agriculture and land tenure, there is no native landlord class to dominate politics and impede social change—as there is in Latin America, India or Iran. (The Murids of Senegal and the white settlers of Kenya are partial exceptions.) Nor does the African elite depend for its power and wealth on the ownership of industry and commerce, as does the bourgeoisie of a developed nation. Industry in Africa is of course almost nonexistent, and most commerce was (and often still is) in the hands of the European trading companies and other foreigners, the Lebanese in West Africa and the Indians in the East. African traders are a major force only in a few countries whose economies are relatively developed, such as Ghana and Nigeria. In general, the African elites are a bureaucratic class—what the French call *la bourgeoisie de la fonction publique.* Power and wealth in Africa are primarily for those who hold government positions; education, aided by kinship connections, is the surest passport into the elite.

In their brief years in power, the behavior of the elites has been seemingly paradoxical. The ideology of social justice and the opportunity to reap the fruits of office have pulled them simultaneously in opposite directions; professed socialism and exploitation for the elite go hand-in-hand. The ideals of social justice, formed under the pressure of colonial rule, have in practice been grotesquely distorted. Yet those ideals retain a disturbing force; you do not find among African rulers the degree of complacency in injustice that is common in Latin America or Spain and Portugal. There is in particular a sharp contrast between the African rulers' performance as politicians and their handling of the economy.

The stability and lack of bloodshed in most of Black Africa since independence have been far greater than many expected. Only yesterday, departing colonial administrators were predicting, often in tones of sour satisfaction: "After we leave, the tribes will be at each other's throats." (This was a necessary self-justification for, if anarchy did not follow their departure, why on earth were the Europeans there?) But after years of independence, the tribes are not at each other's throats. Blood has been shed more than once, but most of Black Africa is peaceful. The ex-Belgian Congo is of course the great exception, one for which the Belgians and other foreigners bear a heavy share of blame; and even in the Congo there was, until 1964, more noise and anarchy than bloodshed. For each case of racial bloodshed (the Congo, Sudan, Rwanda) there are dozens of other places where different peoples live peacefully side by side. When my wife and I left Africa after many months of travel by car in the interior, we were often asked questions like: "Weren't you afraid? Weren't you in danger?" We would answer: "Yes—those Africans are wild drivers." For with few exceptions, the automobile is a far greater hazard than politics. If any Africans frightened us, they were not spear throwers but truck drivers.

A dislike of bloodshed seems to be rooted in the African personality. Deliberate crimes of violence are rarer in African cities than in our own, and are virtually nonexistent in the villages. Between December 1962 and January 1964 the military intervened in the politics of four African nations, three times to overthrow the government (Togo, the ex-French Congo, Dahomey) and once to settle a struggle for power between civilians

(Senegal); they mutinied also in three East African nations. The total cost in lives of those seven crises was less than a few days' work in Algeria during its long struggle for independence. In Togo, unemployed Togolese veterans of the French Army assassinated President Sylvanus Olympio when he refused to give them jobs. With Olympio dead, the capital, Lomé, was defenseless before the bitter ex-soldiers. Yet they did not go on to loot and kill; just one life, Olympio's, was lost in the overthrow of his government. A few hours after his death my wife and I walked the streets of Lomé in perfect safety. The Togolese we spoke with were ashamed of Olympio's killing. "That was not an African thing to do," they told us. And the assassins were not entirely African themselves; they had learned to kill in French colonial wars from Indo-China to Madagascar. Considering the long humiliating history of white rule in Africa, the Africans show extraordinarily little desire for revenge on their former rulers, even where, as in Guinea, the separation has been a bitter one. Despite the bad relations between France and Guinea from independence in 1958 to 1962, despite the Guinean belief (shared by many non-Guineans) that a French plot was being mounted in 1960, despite floats in official parades depicting Europeans beating Africans—despite all this, some two thousand Frenchmen lived unharmed in Guinea through the worst of those years. And the Congo atrocities of 1964 were small revenge, in terms of numbers, for the atrocities committed by King Leopold's Belgians less than a century ago.

Similarly, the postindependence struggles for power have been settled with relatively little bloodshed. In most nations, power has been concentrated in one party and one man; opposition has been eliminated. But po-

57

litical executions are rare, and the one-time opponents of the ruler are usually not even jailed for long. By what amounts to a village palaver within the elite, the ruler's rivals are often taken into the government in minor posts; the opposition is not destroyed but absorbed. Even the more authoritarian one-party states—Ghana, the Ivory Coast and Guinea are examples—are far from totalitarian. The single party attempts in general to include all factions; it does not aim to exclude and punish like Hitler's Germany or Stalin's Soviet Union. African rulers do not, of course, welcome opposition; but where the main motive of a Stalin or a Hitler is to cut down any possible opponents, the Africans' first aim is to bring as many as possible into the general consensus of the party.

Senator Ellender of Louisiana concludes, after a hasty trip through Africa in 1962, that Africans are incapable of governing themselves. Yet independent Africa as yet has produced no regime as baldly savage and exploiting as that of Generalissimo Trujillo of the Dominican Republic, who used to receive Ellender's praise; for that matter, few spectacles in Africa can compete with the late Earl Long, governor of Ellender's own state.

In the economic field, on the other hand, the record of the African elites is far from brilliant. Development was a necessity, the African leaders said when they came to power, so that economic independence could give substance to political freedom. Aid for development has been solicited from the ex-colonial rulers, one or more of the major cold-war powers, and the growing list of other nations from whom the poorer countries can hope to get help. But the new African governments have in fact put few of their resources, whether foreign or domestic, into development. The rural economy has been particularly neglected.

Instead, all too often the money has gone to unproductive showpieces. African capitals are dotted with
these monuments to the elite's quest for prestige. There
are palaces and sports stadia, armies and airlines, traffic
lights, even television stations; sometimes there are hospitals instead of bush dispensaries and universities instead of schools. But usually they are unproductive—and
plainly visible.

Among palaces, the best known is probably the one
built by Félix Houphouet-Boigny, President of the Ivory
Coast. It is rumored to have cost twenty million dollars;
marble is said to have been brought by air so that the
palace would be ready by the appointed date. At
Houphouet's frequent receptions, the guests dine on
china whose cost I have heard estimated at forty dollars
a plate; two villas were torn down to make room for the
palace. Houphouet's is only one among many new palaces in Africa. In Dahomey, whose economy seems to be
nearing the point of no return, ex-President Hubert
Maga built a three-million-dollar palace. Even poverty-
stricken Mali, in many respects more austere than other
African nations, has put one and a half million dollars
into a rather ugly presidential palace. Cement was flown
in for the Mali palace, but, as an engineer on the job
explained to me disarmingly, it was not really as expensive as it looked—Air Mali, the government-owned airline, only charged one-seventh of its usual freight rate
for carrying the cement.

Traffic lights have blossomed in capitals whose streets
you could cross in perfect safety with your eyes closed.
Grandiose sports stadia have been built in capital after
capital; for the cost of one stadium, a nation could have
provided simple sports facilities for all its towns. National airlines are a favorite form of waste. Mali was

59

given old DC-3's which provided its needed internal transport; the government then used its Soviet credits to buy Ilyushin jets which fly useless international routes at great loss to the Malian budget. Madagascar boasts of its internal air routes. When you fly from its capital, Tananarive, to the west coast port of Majunga, you land at a new jet airport. On the way to town, you pass an abandoned airport. The new airport, you are told, exists only as an emergency alternate landing field for jets if they cannot land at the capital. But the jetty at Majunga is silting up and becoming unusable, and no road connects the port with the interior.

Examples could be multiplied indefinitely. All over Africa there is an Emperor Jones quality to elite rule, even in the so-called radical countries like Ghana, Mali and Guinea. The leaders of these nations are obviously devoted to ideals of social justice and economic development, yet their behavior in practice is not much better than that of their fellow elites. (The examples given here are in many cases taken from the better-, not the worse-governed nations. They are chosen to illustrate the points, not to single out those regimes as worse than others.) In defense of the elite, it is often argued that the showpieces they build are necessary symbols that give the people a sense of national unity and self-respect; Africans sometimes say the palaces are designed to impress foreigners. I find it hard to take these arguments seriously. The great mass of rural Africans, those who are most isolated from national life, never get to town to see the palace. What they would see, in any case, is a European symbol that, however much it may please the elite, is of no relevance to their lives. A peasant's attitude toward his nation, and toward his own hopes for the future, will be far more affected by a road that makes it possible for him to get a crop to market than by peering at a jet airliner six miles above his village. As for impressing foreigners, the petty tyrants of Latin America who built extravagant palaces over the past century and a half were rewarded with derision, not respect.

Much of this status-seeking waste is contrary to the Plan. Virtually every African country has an economic development plan. Many of these plans are extremely well drawn, particularly if they are written by the brilliant planners sent out by France. The Senegalese plan is a model. Unlike plans drawn by economists alone, which tend to disregard noneconomic realities, the Senegalese plan is grounded on a study of the nation's social and political structure as well as its economic possibilities. A team headed by Louis-Joseph Lebret, the remarkable Dominican monk-turned-planner, spent eighteen months studying the possible effects of Senegalese society on economic development. The result is a plan that makes it clear that economic development cannot take place without profound social change—a point of view that many other planners appear reluctant to admit. In Madagascar, the planners took a pragmatic view of what are, to many, burning ideological issues. Basing their proposals on the existing methods of traditional society, the planners recommended that agricultural development be organized collectively in some areas, individually in others.

The plans may be excellent, but the results are not. Early in 1963, President Senghor admitted that the Senegalese plan had gone astray. Some parts of it had not gotten off the ground, while "administrative infrastructure" (in effect, jobs and housing for the elite) had been overfilled to the tune of 250 per cent. While administration and prestige projects benefited, productive projects, especially in agriculture, were ignored. Sékou Touré,

President of Guinea, has made similar admissions about the three-year plan for his nation. The story is much the same in Nigeria, according to Wolfgang F. Stolper, the American economist who headed the team that wrote the Nigerian plan. In *Scientific American* (September 1963), Stolper reported on the first year, 1962, of the Nigerian plan in action:

> Investment in the economic development sector was . . . about £9 million below the plan target; within that sector investment in the highly productive area of agriculture fell short. . . . Total expenditure in the social-overhead sector . . . was some £2.5 million above the plan target. . . . Administrative expenses were almost double the projected amount because of the unforeseen amount of expenditure on national defense. . . .

Stolper concludes:

> Although directly productive projects are often difficult, showpiece projects that have no direct effect on economic growth are often easy. The results of the first year indicate a tendency to drift toward them.

Any plan, national or corporate or personal, can go awry, but African economic plans all go awry in the same direction (if they do not vanish entirely, as did Guinea's plan): too much spending on administration, social overhead, showpieces; not enough on production, very little on agriculture.

The reasons are more profound than the plans themselves or the technicalities of carrying them out, or even, as Stolper implies, the relative easiness of showpiece undertakings. African plans go wrong because of the way in which they are born, for they are not African but foreign in origin. The best way to illustrate the point is by comparison with France, whose postwar plans have been extremely successful and whose planners are the authors of most existing African plans. A plan, in Africa or in France, is a series of choices: limited resources will be spent on this and therefore not on that; some people will benefit and others will be hurt. Planning is a political act. When the French plan is drawn, the various interest groups that have a stake in it—management, labor, farmers—use their political strength to push the planners to satisfy their interests as they see them. Later, at least before the advent of the Gaullist government, the interest groups could defend themselves through the political parties. What emerged as the plan was the result of a domestic political struggle, and therefore it represented the relative strength of the many groups that had an interest in the plan's allocations of money. It was not necessarily democratic, since the whole struggle was fought out within the French Establishment, but it reflected the realities of power. If any group took a beating as a result of the plan, it was because that group did not have the power to defend its interests when the plan was being drawn.

Not so in Africa. African plans are drawn mainly by foreign experts invited by the African government; their work is therefore a foreign import. No domestic political struggle tests the plan against the interests of African power groups. Instead, the African government swallows in one lump a plan that is what a group of foreign experts think the Africans should do. But the spending of government funds is the most political of decisions, and when the African government actually decides how much it will spend on what, it is motivated by the realities of African politics, not by the advice of foreign experts. It is then, after the writing and adoption of the plan, that the real political decisions are made. The money goes where the power is, which, in Africa today, means that it goes to satisfy the desires and interests of the elite, not to the powerless peasantry.

Planning, then, becomes an illusion. At times the plan takes on the qualities of a myth. "The Plan will do this," I was often told, as if the plan were a living entity, like those rolled-up documents with arms and legs that you see in cartoons. "Le Plan? Le Plan is only a pretext, a document to be shown when asking for foreign aid," a French planner in Dahomey told me; his logical mind was clearly outraged. (Africa is not alone in this use of planning as myth. Dr. Hugh Tinker wrote in *The Union of Burma* of "the phenomenon of planning for planning's sake. . . . The impression is gained that planning is becoming not a prelude to, but a substitute for, actual constructional work.") Nor do African states have the effective power to carry out many of the projects in these plans.

Plan and reality can therefore go their separate ways. The plan calls for concentration on rural development; the elite spends the money on palaces or airlines or universities. Madagascar has an austere plan whose architects publish reports severely critical of the government; there is no noticeable effect on the government's free-spending prestige-seeking policies. Yet foreigners go on analyzing African governments in terms of their plans. Bringing to Africa their own myopia, these analysts assume that the plan, even if not fully carried out, describes the government's intentions, when, as we have seen, it represents the advice of foreigners and at best the wishes of the government. African governments, like everyone else, are "for" rural development. But wish and will are not the same. The question is whether political leaders are willing or able to impose the sacrifices required by the plan: in Africa, unlike France, that question has not been answered by the time the plan is published.

The Guinean plan was being discussed by a distinguished American diplomat one evening in 1962 at a cocktail party in Conakry. The diplomat, who had just arrived for a brief visit, had seen President Sékou Touré earlier in the day. Now he was praising the plan. Touré had told him, the diplomat said, that the new plan would devote more than half the government's development budget to rural development. The American added that he knew of no country devoting a higher percentage to rural development. "I wonder how much of the money will go to administrators' offices and housing," I commented. "How long have you been in Africa?" he asked, and without waiting for an answer he made it clear that he would not consider my criticism of his own acceptance of the plan at its face value. Perhaps the diplomat was being politic; Guinea at that time was swinging closer to the United States in foreign policy. If not, I reflected later, there was a distinctly patronizing note in his refusal to apply to Touré the standards the American would doubtless apply to non-Africans, or that Touré himself applies to his country. (We need "less whiskey and more independence," Touré said in 1964.)

The same patronizing tone appears among foreign apologists for the African governments, and even among the highly Europeanized African students who are in opposition to their rulers. "Lack of education in economics," or just plain "lack of education," is the explanation they give for the behavior of the present rulers. The students usually add that things will be different when they, who have more advanced degrees, are in power. I wonder if those who offer this line of reasoning realize how extraordinarily insulting it is. It attributes to the African rulers a degree of stupidity—not just ignorance—that goes beyond the bounds of belief. In 1962–3, Hubert Maga, then President of Dahomey, spent three million dollars on his palace, but could not find money for the storage bins that might have saved a large proportion of the corn crop. Did this able politician need a degree in economics to know that the money he put into his palace was not going to produce corn? When traffic lights are installed in such improbable places as Ouagadougou and Cotonou, are the African officials who put them there such fools as to think the lights are really needed? No—the foolishness is not in the Africans but in their observers.

No such strained rationalizing is needed to explain the new rulers. They are catering to their political clientele. If the money is spent in the capital, it is because the clientele of the regime is mainly urban. Some members of this clientele may not seem like "elites" to Western eyes—they may be artisans, lowly clerks or unionized workers—but they are far above the peasantry in status and income and political power. They are the people who supplied the membership of the preindependence political parties, and they are the main supports of the regime after independence. They are the class that is being "taken care of" when the new governments dot the countryside with new (and, by African standards, luxurious) housing for the thousands of new employees they have put on the state payroll—which is why the administrative part of the plan is overfulfilled.

66

Government spending goes to satisfying a profound
need for status, as well as privilege. Since these are the
educated Africans who worked for the colonial administration, status consists of having what the Europeans
had. Not Europeans in Europe, it should be remem-
bered, but the Europeans in Africa, with all their tawdry
feudal splendor; theirs is the example being followed
by the men who inherited their power. "These gentle-
men can no longer even open a car door for themselves,"
a chauffeur murmured to me as we watched Ivory Coast
officials descend from their sleek black Mercedes. But
the Europeans did not open the car door either; should
an African official demean himself by doing what was
below his predecessor's dignity? The new rulers, even
those who are self-proclaimed "socialists," ride in gov-
ernment-supplied limousines driven by government-paid
chauffeurs and live in government-purchased villas
staffed by government-paid servants. All this is exactly
what the Europeans did. When an Englishwoman com-
plains, in Chinua Achebe's novel *No Longer at Ease,*
that Nigerian officials take four-month vacations, a Nigerian replies that this is what the British did, and
should Africans get less?

The sour memory of European contempt for Africans
as inferior beings simply whets the elite's appetite for
the symbols of European superiority. The inner reason
for those useless traffic lights, I am certain, is that they
make Niamey or Ouagadougou *look* more like London
or Paris. Television is of course the last word in modernization, and television stations are sprouting all over Africa. In the poorer countries, like the ex-French Congo
and Upper Volta, television is literally a toy for a few
members of the elite. In June 1963, telecasting began in
Brazzaville, capital of the Congo. In August, when

67

President Fulbert Youlou was ousted, the telecasts were going to just fifty receiving sets. Upper Volta's television will reach only a tiny fraction of the nation's area, and sets will cost more than two hundred dollars: four years' earnings for a peasant, ten months' for an urban laborer.

The elite's need for status shines through much of what its members do and say. In its issue of December 30, 1961, the magazine *West Africa* reported an interview with James Mercer, chairman of Ghana Airways, which has run at a large deficit while investing huge amounts in the latest jet aircraft. This is an excerpt from the report of the interview:

> "We in Ghana Airways [Mercer said] are charged with the duty of carrying the national flag to all parts of Africa and projecting the African personality." Mr. Mercer said there had been criticisms as to whether Ghana Airways was a revenue-making organization or not.
>
> Explaining this situation, he said that the time would come when certainly we would make profit. "The profit that a national airline makes," Mr. Mercer continued, "is reflected in line with the prestige that the country gets in the number of people who come in and out easily, and the trade balance of the country in general."
>
> Mr. Mercer said he knew this was a delicate point, which could not be easily understood by even some of the most intelligent people.
>
> "But," he explained, "this is the policy initiated by Dr. Nkrumah himself, and it is the policy we follow—to bring closer to Ghana all independent African countries, and to show that the African when given the chance can be on his own."

Mercer's statement illustrates how the psychological needs of the African elite override economic logic as well as its own ideals of social justice. The man who really pays for the jet propulsion of the "African personality" is the Ghanaian peasant thirty thousand feet below the glittering planes of Ghana Airways. Yet the personality of the peasant, still rooted in traditional society, is relatively secure compared to the elite's; the peasant needed that money for his income and his health, which are not secure. As for showing that the African "can be on his own," the money wasted on Ghana Airways could have been used to hasten the day of the nation's self-sufficiency.

Sports are another arena of African prestige-seeking. When Dakar was host to an inter-African competition, President Leopold Senghor asked Israel to send—as "aid" —some men to organize the Senegalese opening-day parade. Senegalese participation in an international handball conference was given by the local newspaper, *Dakar-Matin,* as evidence that: "The prestige, the audience that Senegal enjoys abroad are constantly increasing." On August 10, 1963, Nigeria staged a prizefight at which the Nigerian champion, Dick Tiger, successfully defended his world middleweight title against Gene Fullmer of the United States. "Dick Tiger has projected the Nigerian and African personality in the world of boxing today," said T. O. S. Benson, Minister of Information. Not all Nigerians were so happy with the event. Tai Solarin, columnist for the Lagos *Daily Times,* wrote: "With the £120,000 [$335,000] that must have disappeared into our prestige (which, in any case, was there without our stir) we could take 40,000 young Nigerians through a three-year course in our universities. . . . We have gone out of our way to look for a prestige which,

69

paradoxically, must have been worn threadbare by our flamboyant and our most ostentatious search for it. Foreigners must be trying their desperatest not to laugh at us! We would have, were we in their shoes."

No one laughs at housing "reconstruction" in the Ivory Coast, though here the government is actually trying to reshape the African geometry of living into the Western pattern. Along the main streets of villages and towns, the traveler sees mud-brick houses marked with white crosses. This means the owner must tear down the building and replace it, at his own expense, with a structure that meets government specifications. (Significantly, these houses are almost all on main streets. Some marked for destruction are perfectly adequate; on the side streets, hovels remain untouched.) If the owner does not build for himself, the state will simply destroy the marked home; some towns in the Ivory Coast look like victims of a bombing raid. One energetic local official, *sous-préfet* Mamadou Coulibaly of Dimbokro, has made a name for himself by resettling the populations of whole villages on new sites. Coulibaly took me out, in late 1964, to visit one of his projects near Dimbokro. We stopped first at the existing village, a maze of mud-brick homes grouped in the familiar curves and circles of African life. We met the chief, who immediately began to complain to Coulibaly, apparently about his people's forced move. (If they refuse to lead the move, Coulibaly jails chiefs and elders.) We then went to the new village under construction less than a mile away. The men of the village were building their new homes, at a cost of $300 each (more than the average annual per capita income of the Ivory Coast). Of the "improvements" that went into this bill, only a new method of making longer-lasting and square-shaped bricks (mud pressed with a little cement) seemed worth its cost, about $60.

What struck my eye, though, was the shape of the new village: instead of the African curves, it was laid out in the Western rectilinear manner: all right angles, no circles. Here, it seemed to me, was the real answer to the obvious (though seldom asked) question: Why is the Ivory Coast government bombing people out of their homes, at great cost to the state and to themselves, while so many other needs are so much more pressing than housing? Because boxlike houses arranged in blocks *look* European, just as the unneeded traffic lights *look* modern.

Since it is to foreign contempt that the elite is reacting, these governments show a concern with the outside world that borders on obsession. The attention devoted by African governments to world affairs, to the detriment of their domestic problems, brought from Simon Kiba, editor of *Afrique Nouvelle,* the sardonic comment that "economic training of our leaders has become almost as necessary as their statements of opinion on Berlin or the Congo." In reviewing the Cuban crisis of 1962, the Ghanaian press parted company with reality and attributed to President Nkrumah a major role in mediating between the United States and the Soviet Union.

So sensitive to foreign opinion are the African elites that a foreign newsman is more likely to be expelled from some African capitals for unapproved reporting than he is from Moscow. (I was so conditioned to this sensitivity that when, in the Ivory Coast, I read a *New York Times* report from Moscow speculating on Russian-Chinese relations, my reaction was: "How can the *Times* reporter get away with writing that?") African governments are willing to spend freely to polish their image abroad; the Action Group, former dominant political party in the Western Region of Nigeria, paid £40,000 ($110,000) annually to a public relations firm in London, while the regional government's account was said to be "much bigger." Many African presidents and their ministers and officials spend an extraordinary amount of their time out of their countries; their globe-trotting is proudly reported by the local press. These activities are far greater than needed to get foreign aid, or, it would seem, for a reasonable amount of diplomatic business, and there is no evidence that the resulting prestige, if any, has had any useful effect on the people of Africa. Large and expensive delegations are sent to all sorts of conferences; Senegal sent 115 to the Helsinki world youth festival and 32 to a conference of "twinned cities," a cultural organization. And when a conference is to be held in Africa, no effort is spared. In late 1962, the Ministry of Justice in Guinea virtually closed down for months in preparation for a meeting of the Afro-Asian Solidarity Committee of Jurists. Since this was a Communist-sponsored event, some Americans in Conakry were dubious about the reality of Guinea's quarrel, a year earlier, with the Soviet Union. The truth, I am sure, is that the Guineans were just delighted that anyone was going to hold a meeting in their little capital.

Embassies are the most noticeable form of African elite status-seeking abroad. In the world's smaller capitals, housing costs are being driven upward by the proliferation of African embassies; the cost to their governments in scarce foreign exchange is staggering. The governments make little effort to justify in economic terms embassies that in any case cannot be justified by any of the usual criteria: no citizens to protect, no trade to negotiate. (Aid can, of course, be obtained without an embassy.) Some of the examples, like Upper Volta's embassy in Japan, are picturesque. Mali has an embassy in, of all places, North Korea. The Malians also caused a stir in the U.S. by buying a mansion in that old capitalist stronghold, Tarrytown, New York, at a sum estimated from a quarter to a half million dollars. Senegal, which for years argued with Mali about the proper road to "socialism," maintains two embassies with a total of twenty employees in Rome; one of them is to the Vatican —though Senegal is 80 per cent Muslim (President Senghor himself is Catholic). In 1963 President Senghor announced that Senegal would open embassies in Latin America for "cultural" reasons. Ghana and Nigeria compete in the size of their embassies and the lavishness of their entertainment. In 1963, Ghana, which already had embassies scattered around the world, announced its intention of opening an embassy in each independent African country—adding twelve new embassies to the nineteen it already had in Africa. In Belgrade, a couple on the diplomatic dinner circuit estimated that each of the many African celebrations they had attended must have cost the price of a jeep or Landrover; the price is paid in the scarcest kind of money, foreign exchange. When we were entering the Nigerian embassy in Dakar for a huge party, an African student murmured to me: "Fancy parties in fancy houses—that's Africa today."

Elite rule has deepened the already vast gap between classes that existed under colonial administration. "From month to month the difference is increasing between the condition of life of government employees and the masses—especially the rural masses—who, left to their own devices, are becoming destitute," Robert Gauthier wrote in *Le Monde Diplomatique* on February 8, 1963.

The Commissariat Général au Plan of Madagascar, writing in 1962, concluded that "there is no doubt that in the last ten years the gap has widened dangerously" between urban workers and peasants. The gap between elite and mass is already wider—certainly it is more glaring—in Africa than it is in the industrial nations of Western Europe, the United States and the Soviet Union.

African elite salaries are patterned on colonial models, and Europeans usually earned more in the colonies than they did in the same job at home. René Dumont has pointed out that African officials frequently are paid more than their equivalents in Greece and Portugal, class-ridden European nations that make little pretense at "socialism" or social justice. And since the African masses are far poorer than the poorest of Europeans, the class gap is proportionately larger. The African cabinet minister who is paid six hundred dollars a month plus car and villa and servants—plus all too often whatever he can take, for corruption is common in Africa—earns in that month what a peasant earns in ten or twenty years.

The tragedy of the elite today is that it has adopted European ways of consumption without European productivity. The productive attitudes of Europe—the "Protestant ethic" of work, as it is frequently called, though it now has no particular relevance to Protestantism—was not available to the elite. What Europe displayed was not the hard-working society of Europe itself but the somnolent feudalism of Europe-in-Africa described in Chapter Two. Europe brought to Africa the enticing and expensive products of an industrial civilization—textiles, then cars and transistor radios and refrigerators and now television—but it brought none of the productive attitudes and few of the techniques that made it possible for Europe to make and buy those desirable things. And traditional African society, as we saw in Chapter Three, places no great premium on individual productivity. The African elite, therefore, has adopted the shadow of Europe without the substance. Combined with its European salaries, low productivity makes the elite expensive indeed to the African nations. Take, for example, the government stenographer in Dakar who is paid the same salary as her counterpart in Paris. The girl in Dakar produces perhaps one-quarter the number of pages typed by the French girl. Page for page, the African girl is therefore four times as expensive. Now add into the equation the vast difference in the standard of living of the people who in each case must ultimately support the government, and it is obvious that the African stenographer is a far greater burden on her people than is her French counterpart. Such cases are all too common in Africa. Despite honorable exceptions, indolence and low productivity, short hours and frequent holidays are the rule in most African governments.

While the elite enjoys its new prerogatives, the standard of living of the African masses is, if anything, declining. Free spending by the government, without any increase in production, inevitably produces inflation. The peasant living entirely in a subsistence economy is largely immune to inflation, but those rural Africans who buy any imported goods find prices going up. The price of what the peasant produces for market has generally not increased, and since the government has made little effective effort in this direction, his productivity has not gone up either; his income is stable while his costs are rising. Urban Africans have been particularly hard hit. Only a minority of Africans live in cities, outside the agricultural economy, but their number is rapidly increasing. They have suffered the full shock of inflation. Prices have risen, while wages have remained stable or at best lagged behind prices, in the major capitals of Africa. In Abidjan, capital of the Ivory Coast, prices rose 16 per cent while wages were frozen; in Brazzaville, capital of the ex-French Congo, plantains, the basic diet of the poor, rose beyond the reach of their income in 1963, contributing to the unrest that resulted in the ouster of President Fulbert Youlou later in the year.

In an economic sense, much of Africa is less independent now than it was before it gained its political freedom. We saw, in Chapter Two, how the colonial system bound African economies to Europe. This dependence has in most cases increased since formal independence. (Ghana is a notable exception.) Rising prices make foreign goods more competitive with local products; imports then increase instead of being reduced in favor of African goods. While the economy stagnates, foreign exchange earnings from exports do not rise; but the elite imports more luxury goods and therefore there is less for development. For example, some governments even give their employees state loans to buy cars. More government spending and jobs mean a greater strain on the budget—again, less effort can be devoted to development. Deficits, in trade as well as budgets, are natural in a time of rapid development; but most African nations have the deficit without the development. The Malagasy Ministry of Finance noted that Madagascar's government revenue (taxes and loans) covered in 1950 the regular budget and 57 per cent of the development budget; but in 1960, the year of independence, the revenue covered only 84 per cent of the regular budget and none of the development budget. These figures are typical, in

some degree, for most of independent Africa. And while
the financial situation deteriorates, Africa's greatest
capital, the land, is gradually being eaten away.

Agricultural nations find themselves importing more
and more food. All along the West Coast, American surplus rice is in increasing demand; for some nations such
as Senegal foreign rice has become a necessary crutch.
Along these many routes, then, Africa seems headed
away from self-sufficiency and toward bankruptcy.

This dismal picture of elite rule is not, however, the
whole story. Many African leaders have shown themselves aware of the direction in which they are going and
of the need for reform within the elite. "Your privileges, which come from colonial rule, must disappear
with it," President Senghor told the Senegalese elite in
May 1963, and his admonition is repeated in different
form by Nkrumah, Touré and others. Austerity became
a fashionable word in West Africa in about 1962. Sometimes it was an obvious contradiction, as in the ex-
French Congo, when President Youlou announced austerity at the same time as he boasted of plans to introduce television. But even when the will to austerity is
evident, the leaders seem to be in the grip of forces
stronger than themselves, and there is often an ugly
contrast between the *nouveau riche* behavior of the
leaders and their demands for austerity and more work
from the masses. ("Mobilization for the masses and
Mercedes for the ministers" might be the slogan of
many states.)

The outstanding exception to most generalizations
about elite rule in Africa is the Tanganyika (now Tan-
zania) of Julius Nyerere. Under Nyerere, there has been
little of the status-seeking waste, of the grandstanding
on the world scene, of other governments. Unlike his

77

fellow presidents, Nyerere practices austerity as well as preaching it. His official photograph shows Nyerere swinging a pick; Nyerere is directly contradicting, in this picture, the elite belief that work with the hands, especially agricultural work, is demeaning to an educated person. To my knowledge, no other African leader—not even the most "socialist" of the West Africans—has chosen such a photograph as his official symbol. Nyerere also drives a battered Landrover rather than a Mercedes. In nations where the elite is small, and one-man rule is common, such symbols are important. But Tanganyika's independence is more recent than most, and its style depends on a single man, Nyerere himself. Little Togo had a high degree of austerity under the late Sylvanus Olympio, who kept elite pay and privilege far below the West African standard. Olympio was a tough boss. Late in 1962, he ordered the civil service to work forty-five hours a week instead of forty, with no raise in pay; he accompanied the order with the sardonic remark that it took government employees forty-five hours to do forty hours' worth of work. The government employees objected that dock workers, already on forty-five hours, received a bonus for their extra time. Olympio agreed that this was unjust—and eliminated the dock workers' bonus. But a month later Olympio was dead, a victim of his own austerity; he was assassinated by army veterans to whom he had refused special privileges. One of the new government's first acts was to return the work week to forty hours.

Some other nations have a mixed record. Both Ghana and Mali, while displaying some of the most extreme symptoms of prestige-seeking, have also made major efforts toward economic development. (Ghana gets a particularly bad press in the West, where it is deemed

essential to compare it unfavorably with Nigeria, the
United States' favorite African nation. Radicals, on the
other hand, are uncritical in their admiration of Ghana
and unrestrained in their attacks on Nigeria. The simi-
larities between the two nations are in fact far greater
than the differences.)

In these, as in all African nations, progress is impeded
by a series of handicaps. The most difficult of these lie
in the attitudes of the elite itself; we have discussed
some of those attitudes, and we shall return to them in
later chapters. The African states also suffer from some
highly practical handicaps.

Africa "has a clean past and a new start," Tom Mboya
of Kenya has said. The vision of a "new start," free from
the encrusted habits of our old societies, has excited foreign partisans of African freedom who project their own
half-forgotten Utopian visions on Africa. Compared to
the dull middle-aged comfort of the West, Africa seemed
a place where youthful ardor could jump the rails of
tradition and strike out in new directions—and plenty
of foreigners were eager to serve as guides. It all looked
so much easier in Africa. The colonial past had been destroyed. The new elites seemed free to lead their docile
people in whatever direction they chose. The father-
figure who ruled through a one-party state seemed unfettered by the restraints of cumbersome Western political
systems. No opposition party lurked, ready to turn the
ruler out if his measures were temporarily unpopular.
No congressional committee chairmen, no oil lobbies, no
Southern governors stood blocking reform. In Western
observations of Africa (and many other ex-colonial nations) the theme of the wide powers of the rulers, for
good or evil, recurs frequently.

Then what happened? Why have the independent

African governments done so little with their apparently great opportunities? Since independence, the vision of Utopia has come to look like a mirage, retreating ever further into the future. The "new men" of Africa come to look suspiciously like old men, mired in routine, comfortably pursuing, not the Heavenly City, but dull bourgeois security. "We should have rolled up our sleeves and gone to work," a Dakar lawyer commented. "Instead we settled into the safest bourgeois places we could find —and I was one of the first. Now I think we're getting hardening of the arteries."

Are these, in Hans J. Morgenthau's phrase, "bum and beggar" nations, fated by their own national characters to live forever in slothful poverty, putting off effort and progress to a *mañana* that never comes? Many already believe so, and those who hoped for much—too much and too soon—from Africa now stalk out in boredom and disgust. They, and with them many Africans, are victims of their own overly simple view of Africa at the moment of independence. Mboya's "clean past and a new start" are illusions that are widely shared, although not by Mboya himself. New starts are rare indeed in human affairs, and Africa is as mortgaged to its past as are other societies. The limits on the power of African rulers are real, though they are different from the restraints of Western politics. An African president may be free (irresponsibly free, it seems at times) to announce a new course of action, and later perhaps to reverse it, but he is not necessarily free to carry it out. In practice, Africa's rulers are hemmed in by many restraints, some due to the past, some rooted, as we have seen, in the nature of the ruling elite.

The African state itself is a pathetically weak instrument in the hands of the elite. When the European bureaucrats withdrew, they took with them the alien armies on whose bayonets their rule rested, handing over to the Africans a state from which the essential prop had been removed. The results were not long in coming. Once the tiny African armies realized they were now the only effective power in the state, they began to use that power for their own ends in a string of military coups and mutinies in 1963 and 1964. Nowhere was the weakness of the civilian state more painfully illustrated than in Tanganyika in January 1964. Some of the civilian leaders of other countries ousted by the soldiers richly deserved their fate, but Julius Nyerere of Tanganyika is probably the most respected figure in Black Africa. Though his austerity was resented in the elite, he was impeccably independent and many who grumbled also admired him. Yet army mutineers were able to take over the capital city of Dar-es-Salaam, driving Nyerere into hiding, without the slightest sign of opposition; no force arose in support of Nyerere to balance the soldiers. As an ultimate humiliation, Nyerere was forced to ask Britain to send troops to restore his authority, and until they arrived he did not dare criticize his mutinous troops. Later he conceived the idea of getting troops from other African countries to replace the British. The essential pattern of colonial rule had been restored: bureaucratic rule supported by alien troops. There was, even in Nyerere's Tanganyika, no nation on which the government could rest.

Within each nation, the ability of the government to communicate with its people is limited by the extraordinary variety of races and languages, particularly in West Africa. (Most of East Africa has Swahili as a common language.) We were in Fongolimbi, a remote village in Senegal, when a visiting official was to make an address to the gathered people of the region. He stood under the tree that shelters village palavers, the elders grouped on one side, musicians on another. The official spoke in French, for he was from the coast and spoke no local language. He was speaking to perhaps fifteen hundred people, almost all of whom were living out their lives within a few miles of the center of Fongolimbi. Yet the official's speech had to be interpreted into four languages before every group present had understood him. There are Fongolimbis all over West Africa.

Lack of roads, as well as lack of common language, makes it difficult for the elite to reach the people of Africa's Fongolimbis. Once you get away from the capital, travel becomes difficult, and expensive, both in time and in the rapid wearing-out of vehicles. Large parts of most African nations are entirely cut off during the rainy season. Fongolimbi itself cannot be reached by road for almost half the year, and during the other half it is a two-day trip, punishing to both men and vehicles, from the provincial capital less than a hundred miles away. Since the population of Africa is thinly spread, the cost per person of reaching the people of its Fongolimbis is extremely high.

The weakness of the African state makes it impossible to use many of the techniques which African leaders would like to borrow from the industrial nations. We have seen the illusion of economic planning; the African states do not have the power over their own nations to carry out the economic plans they adopt. Such concepts as "socialism," "state control of economy," and "nationalization" are likely to be attractive to rulers who would like to develop their nations in a hurry. The African elites were deeply influenced by the ideas of the European left, which of course generally favored state intervention in the economy; they see Russia and China as examples of the success of authoritarian methods in producing rapid industrialization; and the colonial trading companies of course invite nationalization. To Americans, the idea of state economic control usually spells communism. But the model of state control was also offered Africa by the two major colonial powers, Britain and France, both highly centralized states which intervene heavily in their nations' economic life. In Africa these issues are not so much ideological as practical—a distinction that Russians as well as Americans are seldom able to see. In the industrial nations, one can debate whether the highly centralized state and state control of the economy are "good" or "bad"; in Africa the first question is whether they are possible. Given the great weakness of the state, these methods do not seem workable in Africa. (For that matter, the Soviet administration, which took over a much stronger state apparatus more than forty years ago, has recurring troubles with the operation of a centralized economy.) The concept of "nationalization" loses its meaning when there is no real "nation." This is not a matter of juggling words. In Africa, "nationalization" means putting whatever is "nationalized" into the hands of the elite, to be administered without popular or national control. Under present African political conditions, nationalization is likely to be little more than a tool of domestic instead of foreign exploitation.

The porousness of African frontiers also limits government control over trade and prices. Since there are few natural borders and government posts are scattered, it is easy for the local population to carry on trade across political boundaries. African states cannot afford the huge cost of policing their borders and coasts heavily

83

enough to prevent smuggling. The result is that smuggling frequently undercuts government policy and, especially for the smaller nations, it becomes impossible to set prices and customs duties very different from those of the neighboring countries. Guinea discovered this when, in 1960, it created its own currency (which had little value abroad), imposed export and import controls, and set food prices at lower levels than those in neighboring Ivory Coast, Senegal, Sierra Leone and Liberia. It then became profitable to smuggle goods out of Guinea, sell them for hard currency, buy goods unobtainable at home and smuggle these goods back into Guinea. American surplus rice landed in Guinea appeared in the markets of other countries, and cattle were driven many miles for sale in Sierra Leone. So extensive was this smuggling that it forced the government of Guinea to bring its prices into line with those of its neighbors. Mali, a huge country with a small population, imposed a cattle tax in an effort to force cattle owners to bring their animals to market at an earlier age; many herds were then driven across the border into Upper Volta. In these cases, the African government is handcuffed to the policies of its neighbors and to the actual (if unexpressed) will of its people.

No nation is an island these days, and this lack of isolation presents another and entirely different problem to African governments. In a shrinking world, there is developing an international market in educated people, particularly in science, technology and medicine. Travel is rapid and easy, information flows at an ever increasing rate, education is becoming standardized—trained people are more and more aware of the job opportunities in other nations. The effect on Africa and other underdeveloped nations in the long run may be disastrous, for it is the wealthy nations, above all the United States, that benefit from this international market. The United States and Western Europe are magnets that attract the most talented people from the underdeveloped nations. Short of all sorts of skills, the tropical nations send students to the industrial north, and many of the best never return. They stay where the salaries are high and the lights are bright, and their nations have to do without them (often after paying for their education). A notorious case is that of the many foreign doctors in the United States, who are of course desperately needed at home. The problem is not peculiar to Africa; Israel and even Great Britain have complained of the drain of skilled manpower to the great American market. In Africa and elsewhere, the international market in skilled persons is having the effect of increasing class differences. While the African masses remain as poor as ever, there is a tendency for elite salaries to be judged by an international standard set by the richest countries. How should an African doctor's or engineer's salary be set—by reference to the wealth of his country and the earnings of fellow Africans, or by reference to what a doctor earns in Europe or the United States? Obviously, the second standard means the elite will get higher salaries; it also means that they will be *relatively* better off than their European or American counterparts.

The foreign market in elites undercuts any government efforts at austerity, and of course it diverts to salaries money that should go to development. As the international flow increases, so do the difficulties of the African governments. If the government were to impose a salary scale that is realistic in relation to the nation's wealth and, say, a peasant's income, it would stir up discontent among those on whom the development of the nation depends. They can simply go on strike by staying away, and they can create opposition at home. Already many Africans are staying away; for example, more Dahomeyans are said to be teaching school in France than there are French school teachers in Dahomey. *Afrique Nouvelle* wrote of students who "prefer the tranquility of a bourgeois life in the developed nations to the troubles of a developing country." The magazine advised the African states to "create the optimum conditions" for their return. The magazine said these conditions are "not only material"; but in fact material rewards are necessary to get elite students home and keep them there. Educated Togolese stayed away from their country when the late President Olympio was imposing austerity on the elite; sometimes they took jobs in other African nations where elite salaries were higher. In May 1962, eight months before he was assassinated, Olympio said during a tour of the interior: "It is painful to see how the people of the North lack doctors. This lack is due to the fact that our sons who are doctors, having benefited from scholarships given by the nation, now do not want to come home to serve their country, but go to work elsewhere." "Elsewhere" is often another African nation, so the governments may find themselves competing for the scarce number of highly educated people.

CHAPTER FIVE

Hope and Failures in African Agriculture

TOMORROW'S REVOLUTION, the one that makes the headlines, will doubtless erupt in Africa's seething cities. But the true revolution will take place, if it does, in rural Africa. It is here, in thousands of obscure villages in the distant bush, that Africa must seek its new identity. That search, to which the key is the relationship between traditional society and the elite, goes beyond technology to politics, and beyond politics to the fundamental values of African society.

These realities lie behind the mild term "rural development." Agriculture is the essential element in rural development, and in Africa as in other poor tropical regions there is a continuing debate over whether agriculture or industry should be given priority. This debate is obscured by irrelevant emotions on the African side, and by sterile calculations among foreign specialists. The Africans observe that they were conquered and exploited (and are still exploited in trade) because industrialization had made Europe powerful. Europe (and the U.S. and Russia) are industrial, therefore rich and strong; Africa (and Asia and Latin America) are agricultural, therefore poor and weak. The conclusion is obvious: rapid industrialization is the way to equality; industry over agriculture; build a steel mill. Some economists, for their part, can produce figures proving that investment in industry brings in a higher return than investment in agriculture.

Those who argue for agriculture first are bound to be suspect. From the African viewpoint, it sounds as if these people are trying, by postponing industrialization, to keep Africa dependent on the industrial nations—"neo-colonialism." The colonial rulers, after all, prevented industrialization in Africa, to preserve their industries from competition. If you don't think a steel mill should be built, it is probably because you want to sell your own steel. Or you are thought to be like those anthropologists who want to keep "their" tribe pure and unsullied by modern life. The economists may accuse you, in the words of one of the breed, of being "misled by sentimental feelings towards the mythical 'man with the hoe.' "

Yet the arguments for agriculture are compelling. When the elite's desire for a steel mill is motivated by a search for status rather than steel, the result—as seen in many cases in Asia—is little steel at far too great a price and, for most of the people, deepening misery. Far from being the competitor of industry, agriculture is its predecessor and helper. The industrial revolution in Europe was preceded and made possible by an agricultural revolution; fewer farmers growing more food provided manpower and markets for industry. The Food and Agriculture Organization's Africa Survey of 1962 concluded that "under present African conditions, industrial development depends more on rural progress than rural

progress depends on the development of industry."
Many Africans believe, however, that Soviet Russia provides a contrary model. Stalin's policy—squeeze the
peasants to pay for heavy industry for the power and
glory of the party elite—is bound to attract the African
elites. The human cost was high, true, but it was paid
by the peasants, not the elite. But Russia was rapidly in-
dustrializing before the Revolution, as Africa is not,
and a good case can be made that Stalin's treatment of
agriculture, far from speeding Russia's development,
actually slowed it down.

Among Africa's many needs, the most immediate is
surely for food. Though they are overwhelmingly agricultural, many African nations have to import food. But
imports are only the visible part of Africa's food gap.
The hidden part is the chronic deficit in the nutrition
of most Africans, which is not met by imported food.
Rural Africans need more, but primarily better, foods
—protein and vitamins especially. A better diet is necessary to overcome the inertia, both mental and physical,
caused by malnutrition. Africans who are better fed
will be, or at least *can* be, more productive. Healthier
villagers are more likely to make imaginative changes.
Most important, an innovating rural society may then
take the initiative in overturning the present political
system that concentrates all power in the hands of the
elite; only such a revolution can put an end to the present behavior of the elite. Then, and only then, will
Africa's economic plans be carried out instead of being
shoved in bureau drawers; then, and only then, will
Africa be on the road to a viable future.

The prospects for African agriculture are not, on the
surface, rosy. The productivity of African farmers is
among the lowest in the world, and raising it is not so

89

easy as it would seem. When the Europeans came, they thought that, since African farming techniques were so obviously "primitive," a few imported methods would quickly increase their productivity. In *L'Agriculture au Dahomey,* published in 1906, less than twenty years after the French conquest, the agronomist N. Savariau wrote of the great benefits that would soon result from the introduction of animal-drawn plows and other European tools. Already, he said, things were going very well:

> Since Dahomey has been part of our colonial domain, it has always been a very prosperous country; it is administered by its own means without financial aid from metropolitan France; from its first years the budget has shown a surplus. This situation is due to the rapid development of commerce and agriculture.

Sad reading, half a century later! For Dahomey today is a very poor country, importing more than it exports and able to meet its budget only with French subsidy. The "rapid development of agriculture" never happened; the plows and tools were never adopted; Dahomeyans farm today as they did before the French came. Their consumption has increased with the spreading of European tastes, but their production has not. There are more Dahomeyans for less resources today than in 1906.

Dahomey is admittedly an extreme case, but the record of African agriculture has been disappointing over the last fifty years. Its success stories among peasant farmers—the Ashanti of Ghana, the Chagga of Tanganyika, and, more recently, the Kikuyu of Kenya—are exceptions to a general rule of stagnation. The production of cash crops has, it is true, been greatly increased;

not by better methods, however, but by a destructive increase in the land under cultivation. By now the old African system of shifting cultivation, which required much land for few people, is beginning to break down. As the population increases, the farmers have to reduce the time they let the land lie fallow, and so it produces less. The soil's fertility is being destroyed at an ever more rapid pace. Parts of the arid savanna of the interior of West Africa are turning into desert through overcultivation. To the south, the rain forest is being cut down, reducing the moisture, changing the land into savanna. Tomorrow, if the trend is not reversed, what was rain forest yesterday, and is savanna today, may be desert. African agriculture is living more and more on its capital. Each year there are more Africans to feed, but there is less fertile land to feed them. For many, perhaps most, rural Africans, living standards are getting poorer year by year.

Efforts of various kinds have been made over the years to improve African agriculture: big projects concentrating a lot of money and machines; general extension work; institutional changes.

The big projects typically involved settling Africans on new land, where they were to farm by European methods with the aid of heavy machinery. Their greater productivity would eventually, it was assumed, pay off the heavy capital cost of the project. More of these projects have failed than succeeded; some of those billed as successes have produced far less than they were supposed to. The Tanganyika Groundnut Scheme is the prototype of a project that resulted in unqualified, undeniable disaster. Immediately after World War II, when Europe was suffering a severe shortage of proteins and fats, the Tanganyika scheme was launched by the British government. In the words of F. Fraser Darling, the ecologist: "This was an instance of technically rather than scientifically trained people being let loose with modern earthmoving machinery—the paraphernalia of megalomania." The resulting disaster was on the grandiose scale of megalomania. Machines and plans alike broke down: the projected cost of $12 an acre ended up as $45 to $60 an acre. By 1949, less than 100,000 acres had been planted; the target was 1,250,000. The planted land was producing 200 pounds of peanuts to the acre, instead of the planned 700; West African farmers get three or four times that yield by using traditional African methods. The cost of the great peanut debacle was close to a hundred million dollars—more than the annual budget of Tanganyika in 1962–3. Western nations can afford waste on such a scale; Africa obviously cannot.

The Office du Niger in Mali is another project on the same scale: it too has cost close to one hundred million dollars. Started more than thirty years ago, the Office du Niger uses water from the Niger River to irrigate land planted to rice and cotton. Its tractors do the heavy work, and African settlers do the rest. For many years, the Office du Niger has been ballyhooed as a great success. When I visited its headquarters, in the pleasant town of Segou on the Niger, in December 1962, I learned that it was a strange sort of success. Under its new Malian administration, some of the mistakes of the past were being rectified, but new troubles were appearing. In its thirty years, the Office du Niger has run at a deficit. Its Malian director refused to discuss its losses, but one of his assistants said it was more than one million dollars in 1961 and was increasing because of a fall in production. It was estimated that the Office du Niger would need to double its production in order to show a profit. The settlers had gotten used to having the heavy work done for them by tractors under the French administration. The tractors never were worth their cost, so the Malians were substituting ox-drawn plows and charging the settlers for their use. In protest, the settlers were leaving; their number had dropped to 37,300 from 42,000 in 1961. Yet they had a good life, by African standards, at the Office. They earned around ten times as much a year as the African farmers outside the Office's lands—many of them in fact, hired sharecroppers to do the work and lived in idleness on the difference between the value of the crop and the sharecroppers' pay.

This was one of France's proudest enterprises in Africa. If this is success, one may ask, what is failure? After thirty years and a hundred million dollars, it is reasonable to expect such a project to show returns. Under French rule, the deficit did not matter so much, but the loss of even one million dollars a year is a serious drain on the desperately poor economy of independent Mali, for, instead of providing capital for the rest of the nation, the Office is devouring it. The social consequences of the Office are as serious as its financial losses. By the privileges it extended to its settlers, the Office has created a comparatively wealthy class, set apart from other Malians, where none existed before. Is it desirable to have a group of peasants who earn ten times as much as the men around them? Since the machinery it uses is far beyond African means, the Office has no "demonstration effect": it does nothing by its example to improve agricultural techniques outside its lands. Its operations simply mean that the resources of the rest of the Malian people are being drained off to maintain the much higher standard of living of these privileged few at the Office.

93

No noticeable improvement has taken place over the years in the way these big projects are planned and carried out. One of the rare true successes, the Gezira irrigation scheme in the Sudan, dates back to World War I, long before the groundnut fiasco and the Office du Niger. The Tanganyika peanut case is deceptive, since it implies that with proper scientific preparation it would have succeeded. This is the standard expert's explanation when yet another massive African project fails: technical mistakes. Since ignorance of African soils and climates frequently is not considered a disqualification, plenty of technical errors can be found. Yet the monotonous repetition of failure suggests that the causes go deeper than science or technology. The real "megalomania" is not the lack of scientific knowledge, but the resolutely European fixation of foreign experts and Europeanized Africans that it is economically practical, and socially desirable, to force African peasants into molds cast in Europe. The Office du Niger shows that even a "successful" project may only create little islands of privilege, which are potential trouble spots of the future. The high capital cost of such projects makes it certain that they will benefit only a tiny fraction of the population. The office has cost a hundred million dollars and had 40,000 settlers; at that rate, the theoretical cost of extending it to all of Mali's 4,000,000 people would be in the neighborhood of *ten billion* dollars!

Extension work aimed at the general farming population has also had meager results. Africa is too poor to pay for the kind of dense network of agricultural agents that would reach a large proportion of the population. Most of what efforts were made foundered because of European megalomania and the resistance to change of traditional African society. The typical pattern was for the administrators (European or African elite) to hand down orders to selected villagers: these were the new crops or methods they must adopt. In theory, a few peasants would take up the innovation, find that it worked, and others would adopt it. It seldom worked; changes introduced by compulsion were dropped once the administrator's back was turned. Some of the new methods were not adapted to the local soils and climates, and often the innovation made no sense in an African context. Higher-yielding crop varieties are an example. The varieties are often more delicate, require precise handling and are sensitive to an uncertain climate. So the African who plants them—and who at least survived before—stands a good chance of losing his entire crop. The foreign expert does not then send him a CARE package. Naturally, the administrators seldom consulted the village about its own desires. The new cash crops, the major change introduced by the Europeans, were adopted by the Africans because they needed cash to pay taxes and to buy the new goods traders were bringing to the village; but in most cases they simply switched crops without improving their own technology. Many failures were due to simple ignorance of the workings of African traditional culture. In, say, the United States, technology will spread by the demonstration effect: one farmer sees another doing something new that is successful, so he imitates him. In Africa, this does not necessarily happen. In the south of Senegal, for example, two peoples, Wolofs and Serers, live side by side, farming adjacent fields. The Serers are far better farmers, but the Wolofs have not adopted their practices, despite daily evidence that their neighbors are getting more to eat than they. In the Ivory Coast, when a group of Chinese demonstrated more productive ways of rice farming, the reaction of the local people was said to be something like: "Those Chinese certainly can grow rice!" It is common to hear people tell you in one village that the people in the next village do things differently, and then, in the next village, to find that there is in fact no difference at all. The explanation seems to be that these African villagers see farming methods as an integral part of the culture; the accomplishments of the Chinese, if due to Chinese culture, are not therefore viewed as transferrable to Africans.

Distorted thinking by both Europeans and Africans produced the tractor mania that swept much of Africa, like some form of contagious insanity, in the 1950's. The tractor is a prime status symbol, visual evidence of the superiority of European ways. To Europeans, knowing what mechanization had done for their agricultural productivity, tractors were clearly the way to raise farm output in Africa; to African elites, tractors would also prove their equality with Europe. So, in nation after nation, these mechanical monsters lumbered across the land, destroying the soil as well as any rational economic calculations.

A more destructive import than these tractors could hardly be imagined, and Africa is still paying for the consequences. Tractors proved to be far more expensive than in Europe. Machinery designed for Europe breaks down quickly under the different conditions of Africa. (In Sierra Leone, dust ruined British tractors so fast that the motors had to be replaced annually.) Spare parts are long in coming, and usually an expensive foreign mechanic must be kept on hand. If the tractor breaks down at the wrong time, and parts or mechanic are not on hand, it is lost for an entire season. Already up against a difficult environment, the tractors suffered from being driven by Africans who had no experience of any sort of machinery. When they were not laid up, the tractors were busily destroying the African soil. The topsoil is thin and easily taken away by the erosion of wind and water; below it in many places is iron-bearing laterite that, once exposed, forms an impenetrable and infertile surface. In traditional agriculture, damage to the soil is largely avoided: only the surface is scratched by the African hoe; trees and stumps are left standing, and their roots help hold the soil; crops planted at random, rather than in straight lines, are less liable to erosion. The tractor changes all that. It rips out the valuable stumps and roots, bites down below the topsoil, and turns up the laterite underneath—no native African methods can ruin the land as fast as a tractor. It is an expensive job to rehabilitate African land worked by tractor, and in some places the machines have left a hard, barren surface, like the landscape of the moon, that seems forever lost to cultivation.

The tractor usually manages to supply more of what Africa has plenty of—labor—at a high cost in Africa's scarcest resource—money. Underemployment is characteristic of Africa's peasant population. The tractor, where it is successfully used, may simply increase that underemployment. It is used only for a few days a year, compared to an industrial machine that can be run twenty-four hours a day all year round. And so irrational is the thinking of those involved that repeated failures of mechanization do not discourage the next country from doing exactly the same thing, with the same results. Britain's peanut fiasco in Tanganyika was known all over the world; but that did not deter France from sending its machines to the south to Senegal a few years later to repeat, on a much smaller scale, the British experience in Tanganyika. (Fortunately for the Africans, the peanut fiascos took place before independence. Had they occurred after, editorials would surely have cited them as evidence that the Africans were not ready to govern themselves.) Sierra Leone, which had its tractor mania in the 1950's, lies next to Guinea; in the 1960's tractors were ruining soil and breaking down in Guinea just as they had a few miles away in Sierra Leone.

Worst of all is the effect the tractors have on the thinking of the African elites. No matter how expensive they are, it is not easy for Africans to give up machines which provide the mirage of early and relatively painless equality with Europe. When we traveled through up-country Guinea in late 1962, agricultural officials all told us that their Soviet tractors were breaking down, and most said that mechanized farming was not economic in any case; yet these same men, later in the conversation, would speak of their plans for buying American tractors and selling them to cooperatives. While their minds are fixed on machinery, nothing is done about the many less spectacular improvements which could be made at far less cost. And since tractors frequently come as foreign aid, the Africans' calculations are the opposite of realistic. In theory, the most desirable form of development is that which can be carried out with Africa's plentiful labor supply, without money. Next is that which uses local currency and local goods. Least desirable are projects which require foreign exchange, the scarcest of Africa's resources. Yet the tractors usually are in the "least desirable" class: they cost valuable foreign exchange (even if it is aid, the money presumably could have been used for something else) and they substitute for local effort. And by requiring spare parts and mechanics from abroad, they are a continuing

drain; the African nation is less independent than before
when it comes to depend on foreign machines. Only a
very high rate of increased production could justify the
tractors; but in many cases they tend to depress production by destroying the soil. The tractors are an ex-
orbitant price to pay for an illusion. (There are exceptions. Machinery can be economic, especially in large
planned projects, when, by helping break a bottleneck,
it can actually provide more rather than less work as
well as more production. For example, a farmer may be
limited in his production only by the fact that there are
just a few days in the year during which he can prepare
his land for planting. By increasing the amount of land
he can prepare, mechanization can provide him with
more work, as well as more income, during the rest of
the year. But in view of the tendency to mechanize on
any pretext, any such reasoning needs skeptical calculation before it is adopted.)

Over the years, various attempts have been made to
change the institutions that affect African farmers. The
parasitic colonial trading system discouraged increased
production by taking the profit away from the peasants;
lack of credit at low interest prevents the farmer from
investing in tools or fertilizers or crops, such as trees,
that take years to bring to market. Peasant cooperatives
and a state agency to buy produce at a fixed price, without usury, seem logical remedies. In most parts of Africa,
cooperatives based on European models have failed to
take hold; in the next two chapters we will examine
the Senegalese and Guinean experiences. The idea of
credit as a debt to a distant government did not work
well: most cooperatives quickly went bankrupt. In
Ghana and Nigeria, on the other hand, state buying
agencies known as marketing boards were notably suc-

cessful in providing a stable market at a price announced in advance of the harvest. The marketing boards were set up under British rule, when they seemed to be a useful source of capital for development. Since independence, however, the marketing boards have been subject to all the hazards of elite rule, for they centralize control over farm prices and profits in the state. Just as the colonial trading companies drained off peasant profits to Europe, so the state can now drain the money off to projects that interest the urban elite. Since most of these projects are of no interest or benefit to rural Africans, the peasants are once again in the position of being exploited by aliens. This in fact has happened in both Ghana and Nigeria with the surpluses of the marketing boards, and is likely to go on happening as long as political power is monopolized by the elite.

African land tenure in which, as we saw in Chapter Three, the land "belongs" to the kinship groups is widely considered an obstacle to better agriculture. Since the farmer now plants a piece of land till it is exhausted, then abandons it to lie fallow, moving on to other land, he has no interest in improving the land on which he is working. If he puts money or effort into making his land more productive, it may be taken away from him when the land of the community is reshuffled among its members. Since the farmer has no title to the land, he has no security to put up in return for credit. All these observations are accurate, but the solution that was usually offered in the past—European-style private property—is considerably more dangerous than the disease. Assorted foreign experts have, with the usual European myopia, advised that African farmers should have clear title to the land they farm: this would, it was said, give them an interest in improving it and collateral on which they could borrow. A glance at the history of Europe or Latin

America might have indicated that other results were also likely, for, as the Food and Agriculture Organization has pointed out, the surest way to take the peasants' land away from them is to give them clear title and the right to sell it. In present-day Africa the peasants would quickly lose their land by mortgaging it, the land would fall into the hands of those who have cash to invest—the urban elite—and the villagers would become sharecroppers on the land that once belonged to their community. The farmer would lose that security he now has by belonging to his kinship group. Africa would then be presented with a problem, the concentration of land in few hands, which has cursed societies from ancient Rome to present-day Latin America, and which exists now in Africa only in the few areas of white settlement. Nonetheless, community ownership is a handicap as it now operates, and in some places, like eastern Nigeria, it is breaking down under the pressure of population growth. René Dumont has suggested that individuals be given land title subject to improving it, and without the right to sell. Guinea and Mali propose to collectivize the land, though, as in Russia, this simply means bringing it under the control of the elite, which has neither the knowledge nor the strength to take on such a task. Besides being exceptionally difficult to enforce—fortunately, perhaps, for the African peasantry—property law involves the very basis of society. It is unlikely, then, that Africa will find and adopt an effective form of land tenure till Africans have found the identity of their new society.

Can nothing then be done? The melancholy history of agriculture in the past half century, the many attempts and the pitifully few and fragile successes, have led some in despair to answer that this land and people are hopeless.

Difficult, certainly, but by no means hopeless. While

the headlong introduction of European technology usually does more harm than good, the tools of most African peasants remain, as L.-J. Lebret observed, "more primitive than those of ancient Egypt." Many African techniques are valuable because they preserve the soil from erosion, but other characteristics of African farming are wasteful, and productivity could be increased without danger to the soil. With the pressure of growing population, it is clear also that Africa will soon have to give up shifting cultivation because there will not be enough land to go around; the continent cannot much longer afford to have five or more acres lying fallow for each acre in production. This means that the future requires more production per acre and per man, rather than more acres under cultivation.

Many plausible and interesting suggestions have been offered for improving African agriculture. Here, by way of example, are a few illustrations of what *could*—the verb must be conditional—be done. (Most of these ideas are drawn from the reports of René Dumont to African governments and from African development plans.)

Donkey Power   Tobacco fields near the Niger River in West Africa are irrigated by water carried from the river by hand in calabashes; watering a hectare (two and a half acres) of tobacco takes six to ten thousand hours of human labor yearly. A donkey turning a water wheel, with a bamboo gutter to take the water to the field, would do the work of four men. That donkey would, according to Dumont, repay his purchase price in five to eight *days*—how many investments anywhere produce so fast a return? (When I asked Dumont about that figure, he admitted with a smile that he had chosen the "optimistic" calculation for its dramatic effect. Looking at the donkey "pessimistically," he said, it might take ten to sixteen days to recoup the investment!) Add in the cost of the water wheel, familiar in Egypt since time out of mind, and it would take two to three months to pay off the investment. Donkeys are found along the Niger, the wheel is not hard to make—the technological jump from the calabash to the donkey and wheel is not great.

HAND TOOLS   Most African peasants use just two tools: the *daba,* a short-handled hoe, and a machete. According to the Dahomeyan development plan, a wider range of hand tools could increase peasant productivity from 30 to 60 per cent. These tools could be manufactured in Africa, and repaired by the village smiths, or the smiths themselves could make them. (This might also begin to repair the destruction of village artisanry by European goods.)

STORAGE   The common saying is that Africans spend one-third of their lives working for termites; in parts of West Africa, one-fourth of the corn crop is lost each year in storage. According to some calculations, storage bins for corn (built with local materials) and insecticides (imported, at least for the time being) could pay for themselves in as little as a single year.

PROTEIN FLOUR   One of the severest handicaps under which the African peasant struggles is a lifelong shortage of protein which diminishes his physical and mental stamina. Peanut cake, the remainder after the peanuts are pressed for oil, is rich in protein; the peasants who grow the peanuts themselves suffer from protein deficiency. The cake is exported to Europe for cattle feed. It could be made into flour to feed Africans. Fish is plentiful around the coasts of Africa; it too could be made into flour, which would be much easier to transport into the interior than fresh fish, since it

103

would not spoil.

SUGAR MILLS   In Madagascar, sugar cane is widely grown, and sugar is produced by two methods. One is by grinding the cane, with hand and foot power, between two wooden cylinders. This method, which was considered archaic in the West Indies as early as the seventeenth century, only produces two hundred fifty quarts of juice per ton of cane. Secondly, several modern sugar refineries have been built in recent years. Their sugar retails at a higher price than the uneconomic and highly protected beet sugar of Europe, though the cost of cane is far lower. The main reason lies in the high cost of transportation in Madagascar. Dumont suggests small sugar mills that would cost about $4,000 each and would produce 150 tons of sugar, getting more than twice as much sugar from the cane as by hand grinding. A modern refinery producing 15,000 tons a year costs $4,000,000. Where capital is plentiful and transport cheap, the refinery is cheaper in the long run. But, in Madagascar, the small mills—scattered around the island —would be able to sell sugar at a lower price, for they would buy cane and sell sugar only in their immediate areas. The mills would save Madagascar the heavy investment in foreign exchange of a refinery, and they would provide many more jobs. The growing of cane is now concentrated around the refineries, which discard the unused part of the stalk; with smaller scattered mills, peasants could add a plot of cane and feed the stalk to their animals.

ANIMAL TRANSPORT   Dumont gives the example of a woman carrying three cabbages six miles to market —a common sight in Africa. Each cabbage takes one hour of her time, simply to get it to market. A donkey to carry the cabbages, with or without a wheeled cart, could greatly reduce the cost of cabbages to the consumer and increase the woman's income. Old rubber tires can be used on the carts in place of wooden wheels.

WINDMILL POWER   A cheap windmill of Chinese design, of which only the central axle would have to be imported, could power mills that would grind millet. (Motor-operated mills have usually proved to be financial failures.) Grinding millet occupies hours of the African woman's day; in every village the passerby sees women rhythmically lifting and dropping the heavy wooden pestle that grinds their families' food. It is the African woman, not the man, who is overworked; lessening her labor is more important than reducing the work of men who are already underemployed.

TRAINED DOGS   Since cattle are allowed to roam freely in Africa, the peasants are forced to build expensive fences around their tiny plots of vegetables. A cooperative village system of herding cattle, with the use of trained dogs, would make it possible to grow more vegetables, which are sadly lacking in the African diet.

A more general approach is through the better use of cattle, leading eventually to mixed farming (raising crops and cattle together). It is tragic that cattle, so plentiful in the parts of Africa free of sleeping sickness, are so little used for power or for food. Often you will see women carrying firewood (or cabbages!) on their heads, while cattle wander nearby; the inhabitants of African cattle regions suffer from lack of meat and milk in their diet; it is rare to see oxen pulling a plow. The obstacles to more economic use of cattle are many: by tradition, some peoples raise crops alone, while the cattle herders generally are nomads who plant no crops; cattle are considered status symbols and a form of walking capital, so their owners are reluctant to sell them; the transport and marketing systems are so parasitic that meat, expensive in the city, is so cheap on the hoof that the herder is not encouraged to sell; using ox-drawn plows means a small revolution in farming methods. Mixed farming will not be common in Africa for years to come, yet there are many ways in which the process of change can be hastened.

These are only a few of the many ways in which Africa's agricultural development can begin. The projects we have listed are free of the hazards and disadvantages of the big mechanized operations like the Tanganyika Peanut Scheme or the Office du Niger. Since the projects are spread through the population as a whole, they will not create islands of privilege, like the Niger settlers. The projects are cheap; they will not involve Africa in greater dependence on foreigners for money or technical support. Rather than eliminate jobs, like the tractors, they will create new jobs. Raising peasant productivity and income will provide markets for industry. New jobs in the villages and small industries will take some of the unemployed young men off the streets.

But, even if these projects are found to be technically and economically feasible, they will not be realized soon or easily. If attempted, they may fail just as so many efforts have failed in the past. Innovation in agriculture is an enormously complex and chancy process. It involves a host of technical and social factors; if one of these factors is missing, the whole project fails. The technical factors alone are several. If, for example, the state wants to introduce fertilizer, it may be that fertilizer alone does not produce enough without a new crop variety, and that the new variety in turn requires new methods of farming and therefore new tools. The farmer needs credit to buy the fertilizer, and a market to sell his new crop. No general rules apply to these situations, for the variety of local conditions is infinite. A fertilizer blend or a new variety that works on this field may not succeed on another a mile away.

In Africa, the variety of cultures is almost as great as the variety of geographical conditions. This creates problems of a different dimension. Since agriculture forms part of the tight web of the peasants' way of life, the same idea may be viewed differently in different cultures. In one, it may be offensive to values strongly held by the farmers; in another, it may not. The best way of introducing change varies from culture to culture. In one village, it may be through the chief or elders, in another through dissatisfied younger men, or perhaps women. Credit, for example, is needed, but who should be held responsible for repaying a loan—individuals, an extended family, the entire village? The decision as to *how* to introduce the innovation is crucial: Though *what* is being offered is the same, it may be rejected if offered one way, accepted if offered in another. As in the case of fertilizer, what works in one village may not work in the next.

No matter how much these problems may be researched, those who want to introduce new techniques to rural Africa must be innovators themselves. Since there are no general answers, each such agent of change must have great personal flexibility; he must be able to find his own answers for each situation. This means he must have certain attitudes toward his work, toward the peasants, and perhaps toward himself. Each failure in African agriculture has its own set of reasons, but it is likely that the lack of imagination and real concern on the part of both Europeans and educated Africans lies behind most fiascos on the farm.

Dealing with the unique little world of an African village requires, obviously, knowing that world and adapting to it. Knowing it is not easy. The agent of change has to listen to farmers with infinite patience, gain their confidence, ask questions before he gives answers; communication between them must go in both directions. This does not happen much in Africa. It is a rare expert who has the "feel" of village life, who knows its details well enough to understand why the villagers do what they do. The African technician, like his European predecessor, typically calls the villagers together and tells them what he, their superior, wants them to do; seldom will he find out why the fertilizer does not work on their fields or why they do not want it even if it does work. The technician's unwillingness to listen is the natural result of the contempt in which he holds both traditional African society and, particularly if he is African, people who live by farming. "Africans are children," the Europeans used to say, and who listens to children's opinions with more than one ear? For the elite African, concerned with showing how different he is from rural Africans, to listen to "primitive" peasants without patronizing them may be damaging to his own self-esteem. For the technician, assuming he has been listening, to adapt what he learned in school to a unique situation requires him to be flexible. His aim must be to solve a problem, not to blindly apply a formula he has memorized. But the prevailing attitude in the African elite is quite the opposite: rigid adherence to the rules is more valued than imagination, and status is more important than productivity. Conversations with rural technicians all over Africa turn up people who are repelled—or perhaps frightened—by the notion of adapting their techniques to changing circumstances. Among many such men, I remember a cooperative organizer in the north of Senegal; when I asked him about adapting the cooperative structure to the local culture, his answer was to read aloud a pamphlet—written in Europe—describing cooperative organization. Men who do not believe in change themselves are hardly likely to convince others that change is desirable.

Most of all, perhaps, the agent of change must care. He must want to solve the problems that face the village, and therefore, of course, to understand those problems; he must want the village to achieve a better life; and he must want these things strongly enough to make efforts and take risks himself comparable to those he is asking of the villagers. This is the quality that seems disastrously lacking in most Europeans as well as elite Africans working in rural development. As you travel through the African bush, you stumble on the ruins of one abandoned project after another; the continent seems to be littered with unfinished buildings and forgotten dreams. Yet no one seems to care; yesterday's idea is dropped with a shrug, often before it has really had a chance to fail conclusively. The building remains empty; the grass springs up around the rusting machinery for which someone paid as much as several farmers earn in their lifetimes. No one fights to the bitter end to save the project, or to finish the building or salvage at least the machinery. No one seems to care.

Indifference is more often the cause of failure than is the lack of technical skill, for many of the skills required to improve African rural life are easily acquired by those who want them. I ran across a remarkable example in Senegal in the spring of 1964. At the village of Noto, there is a state-operated training school for young peasants whose purpose is to teach them improved agricultural techniques, which they can then take home and disseminate among their fellow-villagers. The boys build their own homes and grow their own crops during their year at the school. A European technician proposed that the school install four diesel irrigation pumps and grow potatoes. The school director, a Senegalese, approved the proposal, as did higher officials. It made no sense at all. According to calculations made before the project was launched, the cost of the pumps would eat up most of even the best potato crop that could be hoped for. Even if it did succeed, the boys would learn nothing useful, since they could not possibly afford diesel pumps on their own farms; the only lesson would be the negative (and inaccurate) one that you cannot be a better farmer unless you can buy expensive imported machinery. In practice, the potato project was one more fiasco. Since no one at the school had ever done anything like it before, very little was done right: pumps broke down, fertilizer was badly spread. The harvest was pitiful. The boys dug up only a few more potatoes than they had planted. With all that machinery, the crop at the school was smaller than the crops being harvested by peasants using traditional methods—just one hundred yards away. Obviously, the European technician and the school director and the higher officials who approved the idea could have seen, without any great specialized knowledge, that the scheme was harebrained. Indifference is the only explanation I can find in this case and many like it. For the European, it was understandable; it was not his country or people. The same may be true of the Senegalese officials: the illiterate farm boys are not really their people, and they do not identify with them enough to care greatly about their success or failure. It is worth noting, also, that none of the principals seemed to have suffered from his part in the pump disaster; the only victims were the farm boys.

The picture is not always so dismal as this incident would indicate. The African elite is doing far too little in agriculture, but here and there, promising efforts are being made; interesting innovations are being tested. The elite is not monolithic in its opposition to change and many Africans are struggling, under discouraging circumstances, to change the world around them. Two novel attempts to bridge the gap between rural Africa and the elite are described in the two chapters that follow. *Animation rurale* in Senegal and the P.D.G. in Guinea are not the only such attempts in Africa, nor even necessarily the most likely to succeed. "Self-help" in Tanganyika also attempts to bridge the gap, and there are others. The experiments in Senegal and Guinea, each more than five years old, illustrate the use of different techniques in approaching the same goal. Each holds revolutionary implications for the elite and for rural Africa.

CHAPTER SIX

Rural Animation in Senegal

I N SEDHIOU, a remote region in the south of Senegal, a group of young peasants convinced the people of six villages to build small first-aid posts for which the government agreed to supply drugs. The government did not keep its promise; the drugs never appeared. But the project was not abandoned by the young peasants. They convinced the villagers to plant an extra collective field, and with the proceeds from its crop they bought the drugs to supply the first-aid posts.

One part of this story, the failure of the government to keep its promise, is all too familiar in Africa. But other aspects of the Sedhiou story are original. The action of the young peasants in convincing the villagers to build the posts, in order to introduce the idea of Western medicine, is rare in traditional society. Even more rare is the decision of the communities to continue the project, with their own resources, after the government failed to keep its end of the bargain.

The young peasants who set the project in motion and kept it going are men like their neighbors in Sedhiou:

illiterate, they belong to traditional African society, not to the elite; they are not government employees; they expect to live and die in the community in which they were born. All that is different about these young men is that they have undergone a brief experience known as *animation rurale.* The results obtained by "rural anima-tion" in Senegal, in Sedhiou and other villages, make it worth examining in detail.

Senegal displays the usual traits of postcolonial Africa in accentuated form. Its peanut-dominated economy, legacy of the colonial trading system, puts Senegal at the mercy of France, which buys almost the entire crop at a price above the world market average. Because the Sene-galese were encouraged to concentrate on peanuts, the country has lost its former self-sufficiency in food: an agricultural nation, it imports 40 per cent of the grains that are its basic diet. And because only peanuts brought in cash, Senegalese peasants planted the land to peanuts till it was exhausted, then moved on, leaving a desert behind. Cash income rose because of peanuts, a railroad appeared and the great city of Dakar was built; but in its main source of capital, the land, a poor country was made poorer by the colonial economy. In Senegal, as elsewhere, the Europeans were succeeded in power by the educated elite; because the French were here longer, the elite is larger in Senegal than in most of French Africa. But the Senegalese elite does not have a monop-oly of power. Rural Senegal is Muslim, largely domi-nated by the marabouts, notably the powerful Murid sect.

The blueprint for change in Senegal, for making the country truly independent and eventually prosperous, lies in L.-J. Lebret's Development Plan. In a nation of pitifully few resources, the Plan offers no illusions of rapid or easy progress, but a series of relatively small leaps forward. It recommends major changes in the parasitic system of trade which held down peasant income under the colonial economy. In order to give the peasant his true share of income from peanuts, the trading companies were to be gradually supplanted by the Office de Commercialisation Agricole (OCA), a marketing board that was to buy directly from the peasants. In order to supply the credit needed for agricultural improvements, the peasants were to be organized into cooperatives.

But planning, as we have seen, is largely an illusion in Africa because of its foreign nature, and new institutions are often a hollow shell under which the old system continues undisturbed. The OCA, in the Senegalese context, could easily become a tool for exploitation of the peasants by the elite; its losses, mainly due to corruption, are said to have exceeded the profits extracted by the foreign trading companies it replaced.

Animation rurale aims at breathing life into these new institutions by changing peasant attitudes, by changing the social environment in which both men and institutions work. The technique of *animation* was worked out by a small international (largely French) organization called L'Institut de Recherche et Application des Méthodes de Développement (IRAM). The founders of IRAM, like the Lebret planning team, are seeking methods of development that will avoid the human costs of both Stalinism and laissez-faire capitalism. As the name of one of their magazines, *Economie et Humanisme,* indicates, their goal is economic progress without the sacrifice of human values.

IRAM believes that peasants in traditional societies will not change their methods till they change their wider attitudes toward life and society. In a report on

Morocco, which applies equally to much of Africa, IRAM investigators wrote: "We are faced with a population whose traditional psychological attitudes, instead of opening them to new forms of behavior determined by technology, keep them closed in on themselves. . . . Only a profound transformation, creating a totally new climate, can change [their] behavior. . . ."

IRAM's techniques of *animation rurale* are receiving their most extensive test in Senegal. On the basis of the Senegalese experience, *animation* has been adopted in Niger and Madagascar. India and Costa Rica have also decided to test the *animation* technique on a small scale. An earlier effort in Morocco was defeated by the hostility of the dominant political forces. Mainly because of the support of Mamadou Dia, then prime minister, Senegal adopted *animation rurale* in 1959. After a period of experimentation, the program got under way on a fairly large scale in 1961. Although the idea is foreign, and IRAM advisers are still present in Dakar, the real work of *animation* is carried out entirely by Senegalese, under the leadership of Ben Mady Cissé, the austere and thoughtful Directeur d'Animation.

The process of *animation* begins with the choice of a small area, a group of villages, which are similar in culture and language and resources, and in which there seems to be the possibility of quick though modest economic progress. The local Directeur d'Animation must know the workings of politics and village society in the area, which is not always easy in a nation whose varied peoples live in twelve thousand villages, many of them almost totally unknown to the outside world. Once the director, who is usually an ex-schoolteacher, has a grasp of the area, he sets out on a tour to explain *animation*. From then on, *animation* is essentially a dialogue, very much in the African village tradition of palaver, an attempt to establish two-way communication between peasants and elite.

In village after village, the director tells the assembled population that he would like them to choose several young men to learn things that will be good for the village. The young men should be between fifteen and forty years old, experience has shown: if they are younger, they will not command respect in a society where age determines status, and if they are over forty their minds are likely to be forever closed to new ideas. They must also be members of the tightly knit village society, not outsiders who happen to live in the village but not within its culture. This means that they will be men who live by working the land and they will be, almost invariably, illiterate; for if they had gone to school they would have fled the village. They will be linked by kinship to the other villagers and ultimately to the community's mythical First Ancestor. They are men who see the world through the eyes of the village.

The young men must be chosen by the village itself, in the absence of any representatives of the administration, for it is essential they be trusted by their fellow villagers. Only in extreme cases is the director encouraged to veto a village choice. The director explains that he will come back—in the dry season, when there is little work to be done—and pick up the men chosen in his absence by the people of the village.

The director takes the group of young men—two or three each from half a dozen villages—to the *Centre d'Animation*. The Center is a dormitory-style building, deliberately rudimentary so that the peasants will not feel out of place. The director has no desk, by Cissé's orders. The sanitary facilities are, to a Westerner, primitive; but they are simple enough, and easy enough to build, so that the peasants may be motivated to introduce some simple sanitation in villages that have none at all. The group stays at the Center about three weeks. The director lives with them, and except for daytime visits by technicians, he is the only government man present. A deliberate effort is made to keep *animation* separate from the other agencies of the administration, which the peasants view with both fear and suspicion.

The program of studies begins with elementary explanations of the nature of the nation and its government, its past and present, its relation to the village—ideas that are foreign to the young peasants. This is followed by a study of the economic problems of their own area and an examination of what can be done to overcome them. Possible new techniques are discussed. In a typical day, a government official may lecture and answer questions, and in the evening, after he has left, the peasants discuss what he said with the Directeur d'Animation. Near the end of their stay, the young men are taken to a nearby village—not one of their own—and asked to spend the day making an inventory of its resources: wells, crops, animals. That evening in the Center, the director asks them: "What would you do if you lived in that village?"

On the last evening, the night before they go home, the young peasants recapitulate their experience. This is an important and fascinating event, for the peasants tell their story in the natural art form of their culture. In a play, in song, in dance, or in a combination of the three, the young men tell what they have learned, sometimes with a remarkable caricature of the director; a sympathetic outsider is easily moved to both tears and laughter. For the director, the theatrical representation of his teaching is an opportunity to see how much the young men have learned. It is, also, an occasion for him to see the workings of the society in which they live, and, from their caricature, how they see him.

During these three weeks, the methods used are far more important than what is taught, for *animation* is an attempt to penetrate the intimate web of village society and establish a dialogue with peasants who, in the words of an IRAM man, greet the outsider with "hospitality, passivity and distrust." The pace of teaching is adapted to the slow pace of village life; the evening discussion, the most important part of the daily routine, comes at the time of relaxation when the villagers would be palavering under the tree in the center of the village. Lectures must be understandable in the terms of reference of the peasants. Since the aim of *animation* is to give the village a voice in its affairs, discussion must be substituted for dictation. And since only what the village will accept can be adopted, the director often is forced to compromise with conservative traditions of which he may disapprove.

Then the peasants return to their villages. On the day they come home, the village will turn out for a celebration under the tree at which they will again tell what they learned at the Center—this time without outsiders present. In the next few weeks or months, the "animators" will be encouraged by the director to develop, in cooperation with government technicians, a project for their village. Once the project is decided on, the animators will be brought back to the Center for a maximum of two or three days of training in such techniques as harnessing cattle to the plow, simple irrigation systems, well construction, starting cooperatives, building a road.

These two brief stays at the Center are the only times the animators will be taken away from their village. They never receive a salary or an opportunity at formal education, and they are discouraged from seeking government jobs. The essence of *animation* is that the peasant must not be alienated from his traditional culture, and his village must not come to consider him an outsider. If he were to stay away longer, or be paid by the government, or have formal schooling, he might want to flee the village, as so many young men do; and even if he didn't flee, the village would consider him one of "them," an agent of the government. The animator ideally represents the village to the government, not the government to the village. If he stayed away longer he would learn more, but his learning would be meaningless, for he could not introduce new ideas into a society of which he no longer was a trusted member. The villagers are only likely to follow his lead if they consider him one of them. Obviously he cannot absorb much technical knowledge in his time at the Center; but since the technical level of the village is extremely low, there is a great deal that could be done without extensive training, once the village accepts the idea of change. And that decision, to accept change, must be made by the village, according to its rules, not by an outside agency. No innovation is going to be welcomed for its own sake, which is why *animation* is restricted to areas where quick economic progress is possible: where change can be shown to be of value. *Animation* tries to find the leadership for innovation within traditional society, not among aliens. Ideally, the animators are natural village leaders, an elite chosen by the community. As we have seen, the agents of change usually have failed because they came from outside rural society. If they spoke to the peasant at all, they dictated; the alienated educated African official had little stomach for discussion with "primitive" members of a culture he himself had escaped. And the schools built by the colonial rulers served to take the brightest children out of the village—to lop off its potential leadership.

In practice, *animation* in Senegal is largely the creation of Ben Mady Cissé, its director. Any such movement, particularly in Africa, depends on the men who operate it. Austere and incorruptible in an easygoing atmosphere, Cissé is an exceptional figure in the educated elite. In Cissé's mind, *animation* and the innovations it seeks to introduce are not in contradiction with the values of traditional Africa: "We must make it clear that change is true fidelity to our ancestors. Their way of life was in tune with their own environment, but today the environment is different. To be faithful to our ancestors means to adjust to our environment as they did to theirs, not simply to cling to old ways for no reason."

The hangover of colonialism is, in Cissé's opinion, a brake on the progress of *animation*. In the areas where European influence was strongest, African peasants often take the fatalistic view that the white man has a monopoly of the riches of this world; they console themselves with the belief that the black man will have his reward in the next world. So far, the Senegalese have found that *animation* works best in those more remote areas that were little touched by the European presence. There the village culture is still intact; where that culture has been destroyed by outside forces, no new culture has replaced it. In the peanut-growing areas, where European influence was much stronger, *animation* meets its stiffest resistance, both from peasant apathy and from the local power structure dominated by administrators, traders,

marabouts and politicians. Here, where traditional religious leaders and the educated elite combine to exploit
the peasant through the peanut trade, there are strong
vested interests opposing any peasant initiative that
might menace their control. And in villages close to the
city, the attraction of urban life is too strong. In Koutal,
outside the port of Kaolack, there is an *animation* center,
but none of the villagers will attend it; though they farm
for a living they consider themselves too "urbanized" for
animation. Animation, therefore, depends for its success
on "decolonization," on the liberation of Africans, and
especially the elite, from the domination of European
fashions and ways of thought.

Beyond the immediate economic goals of *animation,*
Cissé sees a transformed Senegalese society in which political power will be taken by an awakened peasantry;
the goals and methods of the state would be determined
by the people who are the great majority of its inhabitants. Cissé does not attempt to impose an ideology on
the animated peasants. He believes that cooperative
rather than individualistic methods are more in tune
with African tradition, but each village is encouraged to
use the methods that suit its needs and values. In the
end, he hopes, the peasants once given a voice "will define our African socialism." The word is the same, but
the sort of "socialism" that Cissé sees, based on traditional African values, is in vivid contrast to the woolly
Marxist "socialism" preached by urban intellectuals and
students who are simply copying a European doctrine
conceived for a very different society.

Animation has the advantage that it is cheap and that
it aims at mobilizing the form of capital that most African countries have in abundance: underemployed men
and animals. It does not require extensive foreign aid,

machinery or technicians. Since it is spread out rather than concentrated, there is little danger that it will create islands of privilege, like the settlers at the Office du Niger in Mali.

It also has its pitfalls. Frequently the animator drops back into the anonymity of peasant society and is lost. Sometimes, also, he may become simply another local exploiter. Suspicious villages have been known to send young men of slave descent on the assumption that the government was practicing forced labor under another name; because of their low status, these men had no influence in the community when they returned. In at least one of these cases, the village sent high-caste youths the following year, after they saw that a nearby village had been successful with their animators. A blunder at the beginning by the director can close a whole village to *animation,* and such blunders have been all too common.

In Senegal, *animation* has made its greatest efforts in the fields of organizing human investment and cooperatives. Human investment—the contribution of free labor to projects of public interest—is viewed as a contract freely arrived at between the people and the state. The building of first-aid posts at Sedhiou was a form of human investment. In this contract, the people provide labor (free capital) and the state provides technical assistance and, when necessary, machinery. The Senegalese see voluntary investment as the logical way to mobilize their available labor, for it draws on the African tradition of community effort; collective cleaning of villages, for example, is still common.

Senegalese human investment programs to build roads and small irrigation works have been attempted, with varying success. Even where the projects have not been successful, however, they have shown that the cost of construction can be greatly reduced by human investment. One notable success, the building of a road from a fishing village to a highway, was due to the fishermen's clear realization that there was a market for their fish if only they could get it to the highway.

In the cooperatives, the role of *animation* is to make real what is largely a legal fiction. In the past few years, the Senegalese government has created cooperatives by the hundred. Imposed from the top, without any understanding on the part of the peasants of their meaning or any change in the society around them, cooperatives have had little effect. It is easy to organize peasants under government pressure into cooperatives, far harder to get them to make use of them—particularly when the traditional forces of the marabout and the trader, and often the administrator, are lined up in defense of the present system. The result, all too often, is that the marabout emerges as president of the cooperative, and the trader as the man who weighs the members' peanuts. The marabout now registers the peanuts produced by his faithful as his; the trader continues to short-weigh their produce, perhaps on the same false scales. As before, the peasants accept an exploitation of which they are seldom even aware.

Here and there *animation* has made a dent in this system. In one case, animators mobilized a village to vote the marabout out as president of the cooperative. In another village, the animators, having gained some understanding of how the scales work, were able to observe that the trader-weigher was cheating them on their peanuts; he was fired by the cooperative. In others the animators have been able successfully to use the credit offered by the cooperative, because they had some grasp of the responsibilities that taking credit imposed on them.

In other ways, also, *animation* has had results. Along the Senegal River, among the conservative caste-bound Toukouleurs, *animation* was begun in 1959. Nowadays one finds high-caste Toukouleurs working alongside the descendants of slaves—inconceivable a few years ago. In the Casamance, the non-Muslim region in the south of Senegal, *animation* has helped introduce ox-drawn equipment and vegetable farming on a wide scale. *Animation* among women, which is more recent, produced radical change in a village in the Serer country. Like many African women, the Serer wives spend several hours a day gathering firewood, far from their homes, and carrying it on their heads to their homes, a distance of several miles. After their stay at a center for *animation feminine,* a group of Serer women worked out an agreement under which the state would do the heavy mechanical work of preparing rice paddies, which the women would then cultivate and harvest collectively. With the proceeds of the harvest, the women bought a donkey and a cart, which they used to haul the firewood; since the cart carries much more than a woman can, not every wife has to go gather wood every day. By this seemingly simple change, each woman has saved one or two hours in a day of heavy toil. If only this one innovation, the use of a donkey and cart (or one or the other), were introduced throughout Africa, a great burden would be lifted from the shoulders of the overworked African women.

The reaction of the administration, of the educated elite, is decisive in determining whether *animation* succeeds or fails. When the animated peasants look around with newly opened eyes, they soon see the abuses of the present system; at this point the administration can either crush them or encourage them. In an effort to "animate" the elite itself, Cissé organized a series of "seminars" around the nation in 1961 and 1962. The seminars were palavers between the *animation* leaders and the administrators and technicians in the bush. Superficially they were held to explain *animation;* the deeper purpose was to create an *esprit de corps* among young men, ill-prepared for their tasks, who work under lonely and difficult conditions, in a world where corrupt acquiescence is more welcome than energetic dedication to change. It is easy for their morale to fail. They know their colleagues in Dakar are paid more for less work, and live better. If they "go along" with the existing system, they are likely to be rewarded with a refrigerator or even a junket to France for "training" (which casts a great deal of doubt on the value of such "educational" trips). If they do not go along, they are likely to be harassed (no refrigerator) or exiled to a more remote post.

The days spent at the *animation* "seminar" at least gave these young men a chance to hash over their problems with people they could trust. Thanks to the generous arrangements made by Cissé's office, my wife and I attended several seminars. We found the atmosphere refreshingly frank and realistic. One morning at the center in Koutal, in the south of the country, the young technicians were laboriously drawing up lists of questions for a village inventory—a repetition among the technicians of the village visit that the peasants make during their training. As they wrote on odd scraps of paper, Radio Senegal was blaring the "news" from Dakar. The news was that President Senghor was off on still another ceremonial state visit, that a thirty-two-member delegation was being sent to a cultural event in Britain, that Senegalese delegates were off to international conferences on handball and the peaceful uses of atomic energy, and that Dakar was proudly playing host to a convention of the International Association of French-speaking Journalists, an organization that appears to exist for the purpose of holding conventions. The contrast was striking: from the radio, the status-seeking preoccupations of the Dakar elite, none even remotely contributing to the nation's needs, most an outright waste of time and money; and at Koutal, the young men coming to grips with the realities of village life. The problems of these young men, who are indispensable to the success of *animation,* came out in the question periods after lectures and in the rambling palavers at night around a kerosene lamp. Here are samples from Koutal and two other seminars:

Q. Human investment projects are not carried out the way the speaker says they should be. The deputies never have ideas for projects, and they and the national leaders never show up to share in the work . . .

A. (from Animation leaders). Do your own job well . . .

Q. But if you do, the deputy gets jealous and tries to have you fired . . .

A. We all have to accept the risks of the battle . . . The deputy will talk only to the feudal leaders [chiefs, marabouts, traders] . . . They are becoming outdated . . . Tomorrow we will win . . .

Q. What should we do when a village asks for a school or a cooperative, but they don't really need it or we don't have the means to give it to

them? [Some villages built schools by human investment which fell apart unused because the
government had no teachers for them.]

A. The point is to start a real dialogue between the
state and the community. If this exists, then an
honest explanation will satisfy them.

Q. I reported a case in which the peasants were
being cheated on the scales of the cooperative,
but nothing was done about it.

A. Keep going higher till you get results. Lots of
people, including all of you here, know about
these things, but nobody speaks up . . .

Q. Isn't it unfair for the government to make those
of us who earn low salaries pay the development
tax? [A tax of 5 per cent on income over $120 a
month had just been imposed; a peasant, of
course, earns less than $100 in a *year*.]

A. Our country needs savings for development, but
not one of you in this room has saved a single
franc [general laughter], so the government has
to force us to save . . . Considering how poor
our economy is, and the standard of living of
the peasants, you—all of us who work for the
government—are overdeveloped, not underdeveloped.

In their speeches to these seminars, Cissé and his as-
sociates were pleading for the "decolonization" of the
elite, for casting off ways of thought and behavior
learned under colonial rule. Here is Cissé's assistant,
Ibrahima Sow, in a self-criticism that is rare in its
bluntness:

We who call ourselves an elite may have professional qualifications but we do not have the spirit

and drive that our country needs. . . . We must rid ourselves of the city intellectual's mentality that looks at the peasant with contempt. Our first battle is with ourselves. If we do not change ourselves, we shall fail, and we shall have to lower our eyes when our children insult us. . . . But once we have a group ethic we cannot be defeated. . . .

And Cissé himself has said: "We are lacking the necessary financial capital [for development] but we also are lacking the minimum revolutionary capital among our elites, who are already so remote from the conditions of life of our rural masses. . . ." *Animation,* if it is successful, inevitably means political revolution. In seeking a fairer share in the present distribution of income, the peasants are bound to collide with the powers that rule them. And a rural society determined, in Cissé's words, "to take its destiny in its own hands" is in direct contradiction with the present concentration of political power in the hands of the marabouts and the educated elite. Only about 7,000 Senegalese out of a rural population of almost 2,500,000 have passed through the *animation* process, and only a small minority of these are truly "animated." They have affected others in some cases, but the balance of power is still tilted in favor of the marabouts and the elite. So the supporters of *animation* hope that any showdown clash can be put off till their movement is too strong to be crushed.

In a society following the laws of economic determinism, *animation* would doubtless have already been destroyed (if it had ever begun) as a menace to the ruling class. Africa is not like that. It is part of the peculiar nature of African politics today that contradictory ideals and self-interest coexist within the same system: the ideal of social justice tempers the reality of exploitation. In the case of the marabouts, the leaders of *animation* have been careful in their approach to the strongholds of the Murid sect, which unites more than 500,000 Senegalese under the control of the M'Backé family. They sought as their first animators members of households known for their loyalty to the family; these men then defended *animation* against its critics as being concerned purely with production. Production is something the Murids understand and appreciate—the ruling family's income is based on peanuts—so they have no cause as yet to complain. Falilou M'Backé, the Grand Marabout of the Murids, told me that there is a "perfect symbiosis" between *animation* and Muridism. He could have halted *animation* among his faithful with a snap of his fingers, but he has not done so. Secure in the fidelity of their people, it is probable that the marabouts do not yet see any threat to their position.

The marabouts, however, are not, as Ibrahima Sow once remarked, "the most wicked ones." The "most wicked ones," the natural opponents of *animation,* are the present ruling elite. This educated class, whose performance in power and alienation from their people we have seen in earlier chapters, has more reason than the marabouts to feel directly threatened by any gain in political power on the part of the peasants. The marabouts, in return for their exploitation of the faithful, at least offer them secure leadership in this world and the hope of heaven in the next. The elite, culturally a world away from the peasants, can offer neither; if they should, as members of the elite often recommend, "smash the marabouts," they would, like the Europeans before them, have little to offer the peasants in return. Yet the elite has not as a group offered outright opposition to *animation;* opposition only comes from individuals whose interests are directly affected: a deputy, for example, whose income from the peanut trade has been lowered by a successful cooperative. Here again *animation* benefits from the myth of progress that is part of independent Africa's intellectual equipment: in practice the myth may be violated, but it cannot be openly denied. Perhaps also it is difficult for the elite, which rightly credits itself with leading Africa to independence, to see just how excessive its present privileges are.

The future of *animation* is still uncertain. A balance sheet of its results is exceedingly hard to draw up, for *animation* consists of hundreds of obscure struggles, of decisions made or unmade, in isolated villages deep in the bush. In the ministries in Dakar, few know the outcome of most of those struggles. Even in the village itself, it is not easy to find out what has happened, for the villagers are reluctant to reveal themselves to outsiders. The very meaning of words may be altered to suit what the villagers believe to be the outsiders' desires. In one village, a study mission from Dakar was told that, thanks to *animation,* the villagers were farming a "collective" field. Only by actually visiting the field and by patient questioning did the outsiders find out that the collective field was in reality the field of the young man who had gone to the Centre d'Animation. He was farming it alone, just as he had before his experience of *animation.* Nothing at all had changed, and the villagers knew it. They called it the "collective" field in the hopes that the word would satisfy the outsiders and induce them to go away.

By 1964, *animation* was suffering from an obvious loss of momentum. Its successes were isolated incidents.

The spirit of innovation was not spreading from the animators to the rest of the peasants; instead of putting pressure on the elite, most of the animators seemed to be disappearing back into the apathetic mass. When I traveled around Senegal in the spring of 1964, I found a general air of pessimism about *animation*. The troubles seemed rooted in the elite, in the local directors and technicians. Here, as in so many cases in Africa, they seemed uninterested in their jobs. One local director, I was told, had scheduled the *animation* training session during Ramadan, the Muslim holy month in which people fast from sunrise to sunset. Choosing Ramadan, the worst time of the year for any kind of activity, can hardly be explained by ignorance. As in the diesel pump fiasco, described in the previous chapter, the only explanation that makes sense is that the director just did not care whether *animation* succeeded or not. Other directors take on projects that are obviously beyond the capabilities of the peasants and technicians. One such was the building of a road, near St. Louis in the north, to connect swamp villages to the main highway. The villagers were to provide free labor, the state technical aid. The project was far too big. It bogged down repeatedly—the state failed to deliver its promised help, the peasants got discouraged and quit. It was still going, in spring of 1964, only because of the presence of three United States Peace Corps volunteers. Whenever work stopped, the volunteers badgered both technicians and peasants until it got started again. The volunteers were acting as the agents of change, though they knew little about the technology of road building; they were the essential link between the elite and the peasants. They kept moving a project that the technicians and the director of *animation*—and the peasants—were willing to abandon. In that

difference of attitudes between the volunteers and the
elite lies the explanation of the failures of *animation*.

Cissé's dedication does not reach down to the local
Centre d'Animation, where the struggle to change rural
Africa will be won or lost. The inability of Cissé to
animate those members of the elite who work for him
mirrors the general state of the elite. Like Cissé, President Senghor cannot stir the elite; the speeches in which
he attacks their behavior fall on deaf ears. The atmosphere of discouraged apathy was general. In villages and
towns all over Senegal, I found officials who, after making a brief effort, had lapsed into indolence and now
blamed their inactivity on their superiors in the capital.
In the town of Kolda, I visited a hospital run by a doctor who, I have been told in Dakar, was dedicating his
life to rural Africa. I could see at a glance that the hospital was a mess. The doctor knew it, and he knew that
his neglect was obvious to any visitor. We had barely
been introduced when the doctor, staring at the floor,
launched into a bitter harangue: "Those people in the
ministry in Dakar are all thieves and idiots . . . so why
should I wear myself out?"

Why indeed? An elite lacking in "revolutionary capital" is not going to lead the productive revolution that
rural Africa needs. In their offices in distant towns, the
technicians spoke of the need of *animation ministérielle:*
without vigorous and innovating leadership from the
ministers at the top, they were unwilling—or afraid—to
do anything. At the summit of the Senegalese power
structure, Senghor and Cissé also pleaded for *animation
ministérielle*. Yet nothing was happening. Neither the
elite nor the peasants seemed to have the faith that they
could really change their environment, and lacking that
faith, they refused to take the risks involved in innova-

tion of any kind.

The brief history of *animation* holds important lessons. Its successes show that the African village community is not closed to progress, that its culture does not have to be destroyed before new ways can be introduced. Where that culture is still vital, villagers can be persuaded that, in Cissé's words, "change is true fidelity to our ancestors." After all, the First Ancestor was himself an innovator, for he created the community and framed its laws. The failures of *animation,* on the other hand, show once more that the main block to progress is the profound lack of faith of the ruling elite. They have lost the old faith of traditional Africa, and they have no new faith to replace it. They have not won what Cissé's assistant, Ibrahima Sow, called that "first battle with ourselves."

CHAPTER SEVEN

Sékou Touré and the Parti Démocratique de Guinée

CONAKRY, the capital of Guinea, is a shabby and charming town whose atmosphere is unlike that of most African cities. Like Lisbon in World War II, it is a city of rumor, intrigue and blackmarketing, in which mysterious foreigners eye each other suspiciously against a cheerful African background. Shortages are frequent, and people seek out the smuggler who has rice or peanut oil or auto parts. In the bar of the fancy Hotel de France, a Swiss businessman lurks with a deal in his brief case, and everyone speculates about the newly arrived Israeli who may be buying diamonds. On the beach at the end of town, the Americans and the Russians have staked out their separate plots of sand; both wonder what the Chinese Communists, remote in their embassy, are doing. On the next spit of land, the statues of former French governors—piled up there by the Guineans after independence—stare out across the cove at the new foreigners who have come in their wake.

The Guinean scene is dominated by the dynamic figure of Sékou Touré. President Touré's handsome face

appears everywhere, in portraits on the flaking walls of
government offices, even on the printed dresses of the
Guinean women when they turn out to dance in the
streets on state occasions (shocking, it appears, such souls
as George H. T. Kimble, the American geographer.
". . . there must surely be more becoming ways of pro-
claiming one's loyalty to a leader than by wearing cotton
cloth so patterned with his image that the wearer must
needs sit on it," Kimble wrote with prim disapproval in
Tropical Africa. As we watched the Guinean women
paying good-natured tribute to their handsome President and to the pleasures of the dance, we wondered
how anyone other than a hard-shell missionary could
possibly find their dress not "becoming"). Unchallenged
as leader of his own country, Touré in his early forties
is a popular figure in the rest of Africa because of his
dramatic defiance of Charles de Gaulle in 1958; under
Touré's leadership, Guinea alone among France's colonies took immediate independence by voting *non* in
de Gaulle's historic referendum. Touré was described
once as "the second most important man" in the neighboring Ivory Coast, and in distant Madagascar a journalist commented that "compared with Guinea, we are still
children, dependent on Papa de Gaulle." When in 1961
a young Senegalese sociologist, Jean-Pierre N'Diaye,
took an opinion survey of African students in Paris, he
found Touré by far the most popular of African leaders.
In answer to the question: "Which African do you most
admire and respect?" 124 of 310 students named Touré.
He was followed far behind by Lumumba, then already
dead, with 81 votes, and Nkrumah, with 45. Students
from English-speaking Africa would have doubtless
voted differently, but Touré far outdistanced other
French-speaking leaders. Among the reasons given for

135

their choice, this one, from a student from Upper Volta, is typical: "He was able to say 'non' at a time when it would have been easier to say 'oui.' "

The world is interested in Guinea because of the cold war, and in Touré because he defied de Gaulle. But this little country and its leader will retain our interest here on quite different grounds. For Guinea is engaged in an experiment in nation-building that, like *animation rurale* in Senegal, illustrates both the problems and the potential of independent Africa.

The Guinean experiment is the social policy of the Parti Démocratique de Guinée, the dominant force in a one-party state. Its aims are those of *animation:* to stimulate people living within the bonds of traditional society to want progress, to take responsibility for their destiny, to demand their due from their rulers. The means are different. Where *animation's* appeal is mainly economic, that of the PDG is political. *Animation* concentrates on small groups, the PDG appeals to the nation as a whole. Though both use the technique of palaver, the tone of the PDG is feverish compared to that of *animation*. But since their ultimate goals are similar, both the PDG and *animation* have run up against the same obstacles in the attitudes of the ruling elite.

In Guinean political theory, a highly centralized state should control the economy; a mass-based political party, the PDG, should in turn control the state. By "socializing" the economy, the state was to break the colonial grip on the nation. The elite inevitably would operate the state, but they would be under the control of the PDG. In every conflict between the two, the party was to dominate the state, for the party was to be the "motor," the "brain," of the revolution.

The PDG has been a mass party from its beginning.

In preindependence elections, the party's broad organization enabled it to defeat its rivals despite the hostility of the French administration. Now it has a local unit in virtually every village and every neighborhood of the towns: a total of about 7,000 local party committees. In December 1962, Camara Daouda, the PDG permanent secretary, told me that one and a half million Guineans had bought membership cards that year at a hundred francs (forty cents) each. That claim may be vastly exaggerated—it would include virtually every adult in the population—but there is no doubt that the PDG makes every effort to get the entire nation in its ranks. On Thursday evenings, when PDG meetings are held all over the country, the party uses all sorts of pressure, including ungentle shoving, to make people attend. The party theoretically is democratically organized, though in practice there are few contests within it. All its office holders, from the village committees to the governing Bureau Politique National (BPN), are regularly put up for re-election.

The party's organization reflects Touré's deep distrust of the elite. More than most African leaders, Touré has been consistently harsh in his judgment of the educated elite, whom he considers "alienated" and still "colonized." In 1962, Touré commented that "many perverted intellectuals give themselves the title of 'cadres of the revolution,' and consider that the number of their university diplomas is the criterion of their social utility." In the same speech, he mocked "those who speak of mechanizing the means of production but are themselves incapable of changing a light bulb." Accordingly, Touré has tried to set up safeguards against control of the party by the elite. He has forbidden the *commandants de region*—the most important administrative officials—to hold responsible positions in the party hierarchy. This, in theory, is to guarantee that the party will remain in the hands of the people. The nature of membership in the party is what distinguishes the PDG from a Communist party. The party's organization, the doctrine of party supremacy over the state, the Marxist vocabulary that Touré often uses, all these have led many to equate the PDG with Communist party rule. When the BPN is referred to as the "politbureau," the translation is accurate, but the impression is misleading. For in contrast to the PDG, a Communist party is an elite party. It deliberately restricts its membership to a tiny fraction of the population, and thereby puts a monopoly of political and economic power into the hands of a small self-recruiting aristocracy. By including everyone in the party, the PDG is trying to do precisely the opposite: take political power from the elite and give it to the general population.

In view of Touré's opinion of the elite, it is not surprising that he eventually came in conflict with Guinea's small intellectual fringe. These men, a small band of secondary school teachers, realized they did not have either the prestige or the pay in Guinea that they would have had in other African nations. An elite party along Communist lines would have suited their interests better than the PDG. In July 1961, Touré warned the teachers against trying to form a "privileged caste of intellectuals." By October, the intellectuals were muttering that Guinea "could not remain neutral in the Cold War" (meaning that she should side with the Soviet Union); in November they circulated a memorandum criticizing the government for refusing the teachers a raise. The government arrested the teachers. Their students, the privileged boys and girls who attend the *lycée* in Conakry, went on strike and demonstrated against the government. Touré reacted harshly. In a deeply symbolic act, he sent the illiterate young men of the party's youth arm, the Jeunesse du Rassemblement Démocratique Africain, to smash the strike of the elite students. (Similarly, President Nkrumah of Ghana sent his lower-class Builder's Brigades to make a show of strength before the intellectuals at the University of Ghana, in February 1964.) The Russian Ambassador, Daniel Solod, was expelled on suspicion of conspiring with the teachers, who were sentenced to death (but at this writing apparently have not been executed). When Guinean students abroad declared their "solidarity" with the Soviet Ambassador, Touré summoned them home for interrogation. Touré caustically remarked: "If we say that the Guinean students in France are not yet decolonized, that they have not yet worked out their own conversion, it is because they themselves constantly offer proof of this. . . . Its characteristic marks [are] a gross overestimation of the students' role in the Guinean Revolution, and an equally gross underestimation of the Guinean peoples' revolutionary struggle. . . ."

The teachers' plot, involving only a handful of members of the elite, did not impede the fundamental task of the PDG. This was to make contact with and animate the mass of people who were indifferent to government and thought of themselves by race or clan or village rather than by nation. In a society dominated by men and by the elders, the PDG pitched a special appeal to women and youth. On each ten-member party committee, three places are reserved for women and two for members of the party's youth movement, the JRDA. Touré speaks often of improving the status of women, and unlike most leaders of Muslim countries, he has made it clear he disapproves of polygamy, though he has not tried to outlaw it (which would be impossible to enforce). The minimum age for marriage has been raised from thirteen to seventeen. Two women are members of the BPN, and many are mayors of villages—in these positions they theoretically have men under their authority. Some, also, are in the police, a job of obvious authority. More and more girls are going to school; from there they can enter the elite in their own right.

Through the JRDA, young men and women are given a place of respect that is in direct contradiction to the customs of traditional African society. The party seems to think that the youth rather than their elders will really accept the party's faith that loyalty belongs to the nation before the clan or race. (But we heard no reports in Guinea of the denunciations of parents by children that were common under both Hitler and Stalin.) Besides public honors, the PDG has given youth a voice in an issue of crucial importance: the dowry. With educated boys far outnumbering educated girls, the bride price has risen till some young men cannot afford to be married. (In Senegal, lip service is paid to youth—but it was the religious leaders who were asked to regulate the bride price.) The party's activities among women and youth could in theory be revolutionary. It is they, and particularly the overworked women, who have a personal stake in changing their lives. For the African man who exploits his wife or wives, change is not necessarily attractive. This point was often missed in colonial times by agricultural extension agents who made their approaches to the head of the household: since his wives and sons did all the work anyway, the man's interest in innovation was at best theoretical.

In its role as animator, the PDG was also to be the

mainspring of human investment. The idea of human investment was widely publicized in Guinea in the first years of independence, more so than in other African countries. Human investment—free labor on projects of community interest—was to supply the capital that Guinea lacked; and the party, through its local committees, was to pick the projects and enlist the people to carry them out.

These were the theories on which the Guinean experiment was launched in October 1958, when Touré said "non" to de Gaulle. Like *animation rurale* the theory is extremely attractive: courageous little Guinea seemed to have chosen a truly African path to progress. But in practice the course of Guinea since 1958 has been disappointing indeed.

In the first two years, Guinea set up a highly centralized state apparatus that was to bring the nation's economy, like its politics, under African rather than colonial control. European trading companies and banks were either nationalized or driven out. The export and import trades were made state monopolies. State stores were opened in the interior, and prices were regulated by the state. These were the institutions Touré referred to in 1959 when he said: "We intend to replace them [the colonial commercial system] with new structures perfectly adapted to a constant economic evolution and to a continual harmonization of this evolution." In March 1960, Guinea substituted its own currency, the Guinean Franc, for the CFA franc that had circulated in all of ex-French West Africa. (The durable initials CFA have an entertaining history. Originally they stood for "Colonies Françaises d'Afrique." With the 1958 referendum and the granting of internal autonomy, this was changed to "Communauté Franco-Africaine." When de Gaulle's Communauté fell apart, the name of the currency was changed still again, to "Communauté Financière Africaine.") The Guinean Franc was seen as the final blow to colonialism. "The colonial franc is dead. . . . Long live the Guinean Franc—condition, instrument and symbol of our economic liberation!" the government proclaimed. By 1961, only one major foreign economic interest remained in Guinea: the FRIA aluminum plant, owned by the international aluminum interests. Through barter agreements, the Soviet Union by then had a stranglehold on Guinea's foreign trade, but the internal economy was truly in Guinean hands. The state had created the institutions it wanted to carry out a three-year plan calling for a major effort in agricultural production, which was to rise by 10 per cent a year.

The failure that resulted was grotesque. In its first five years, Guinea produced a rich store of picturesque anecdotes that delighted foreigners, particularly if they were hostile, and Touré in 1962 complained of the "reputation of anarchy" that his country had acquired. Philippe Decraene of *Le Monde* chose to title a series on Guinea after four years: "Journey to the End of the Night." Decraene, whose writing usually follows the official French line, was a biased observer; but he was able to find all too much evidence for the picture he drew of a nation falling to pieces. Stories of scandal and monumental blunders circulated. Public services decayed, consumer goods disappeared, smuggling and black marketing became common. The cost of living rose, particularly in Conakry. The waste of expensive materials was (and is) appalling. Hundreds of unassembled prefabricated houses rotted away because they were left without shelter during the rainy season; both imports and exports rotted on the clogged and chaotic docks of

Conakry. In late 1962, we drove through much of the interior. Everywhere we saw rusting farm machinery and trucks, many obviously new; in a truck graveyard in Conakry, I counted thirty abandoned trucks, many hardly used. It was depressing to think of the loss to the people of Guinea that these wasted machines represented.

By 1962, it was clear that Guinean management of the economy was more costly to its people than colonial exploitation had been. The consumer was worse off: many goods simply could not be found; others had become more expensive. Like the OCA in Senegal, but on a far larger scale, the state trading monopolies were proving a poor substitute for the colonial trading companies—they cost the nation losses of at least forty million dollars.

Nor were these losses balanced by a rise in production. Statistics in Guinea are even scantier and less reliable than elsewhere in Africa, but it seems that productivity dropped over the first four years. Banana and pineapple exports declined, because the state organization could not get them to the docks on time and could not supply insecticides when they were needed. The three-year plan simply disappeared. No attempt was made to carry out such productive projects as a factory for light agricultural tools. In 1959 René Dumont made a series of proposals for improving Guinea's agriculture; none was spectacular, all seemed to be within the state's technical and economic means. In late 1962 I asked about many of Dumont's proposals in different regions of Guinea: I was unable to find a single one that had been seriously attempted, though far more money had been wasted than his ideas would have cost.

While the productive economy was starved, Guinea

was building the familiar prestige showpieces. The East Germans built the impressive Imprimerie Patrice Lumumba, the "most modern printing plant in Africa," according to the press releases. A printing plant was hardly a high-priority need for Guinea, which already had one, and P. Lumumba's capacity was far beyond the nation's needs—even its potential needs. Now most of that fine German equipment lies unused, and the plant in 1963 was running at about 5 per cent of capacity. That favorite status symbol, a national airline, appeared, with Ilyushin-18 jets for nonexistent passengers—while the railroad fell apart. The Russians built a sports stadium and a 100-kilowatt radio transmitter (far in excess of the power needed to reach all of Guinea); they started also on a fancy polytechnical institute and a hotel. Communist tanks even appeared for the Guinean army; they are handy for parades, but it is doubtful whether they could ever make it to the nation's frontiers.

In the countryside, the Guineans have also built prestige showpieces, though on a more modest scale. We ran across a typical example in N'Zérékoré, a provincial center tucked away in the remote side pocket of Guinea, near the borders of both Liberia and the Ivory Coast. On our arrival in N'Zérékoré, we called on the acting commandant, the chief administrator of the region. With the usual gracious hospitality of Africa, the acting commandant, Ibrahima Diallo, offered to take us on a tour of N'Zérékoré. We did not ask to see anything in particular; the commandant said he would show us "the accomplishments of our Revolution." This is what he showed us:

The mansion built for the commandant. Except for the commandant's office building, also new, the

residence was the largest building we saw in
N'Zérékoré.

The presidential villa, on a hill overlooking the
town, for Sékou Touré to occupy when he is there.
When Touré is not there—all but a few days a year,
that is—the luxuriously appointed villa stands
empty. Two six-room guest houses, with two bath-
rooms in each, are provided "for the President's
guests." On the hill above the villa, the commandant is laying out a park—"for tourists"—with
little gravel paths bearing such names as "Boule-
vard du Peuple" and "Avenue P. Lumumba."

A new hotel under construction. This, too, is
"for tourists," though tourists are rare indeed in
this town, three days' drive from Conakry by Landrover over bad roads. N'Zérékoré already has a
hotel. It is pretty grim but would be habitable if it
were cleaned up. In the new hotel, each of twenty
rooms will have a bath; there will be a park in
front; in back there will be motel-style cabins "for
couples who want privacy."

European-style housing for the Garde Répub-
licaine that mans the borders against an unlikely
foe. "Since September, 1961, we have built thirty-
six units," the commandant said.

We were impressed by the innocence with which the
commandant displayed these status symbols. Nothing
he showed us was of any conceivable value to the people
of N'Zérékoré; it was all in stark contradiction to the
professed ideals of the "Revolution." Yet this did not
bother the commandant. It did not seem to occur to
him that we would be shocked by what he showed us.
He did not bother to show us the secondary school and

the hospital that have also been built since independence. When we mentioned this to a Bulgarian doctor who staffs the hospital with another Bulgarian and an Italian, he said: "Maybe he's ashamed of the hospital—he certainly should be." All three doctors were bitter at what they considered to be the indifference of the local administration: the hospital has no running water, and until just before our visit, had had no electricity, although there is electricity in N'Zérékoré. "The hospital is the last of the commandant's interests," the Italian doctor commented.

What happened to Guinea? The state was obviously not up to the tasks assigned to it. Guinea had neither the trained personnel nor the communications needed to operate a centralized economy. (The state trading monopolies were run by men who, the day before, had been clerks.) So the new institutions collapsed under the impossible burdens put on them. The issue is not the familiar one of the ideological merits of state control versus free enterprise: what was possible in, for example, the centralized Britain of 1940 to 1950, under both Tories and Labor, was plainly impossible in Guinea. "Nationalization" was a deceptive slogan in a country that was not yet a nation. The Guinean leaders and their foreign sympathizers—both equally obsessed by European standards—failed to see that "nationalization" in Guinea meant putting the economy in the hands of the elite. And the elite, inevitably, used the country's resources to satisfy their own desires.

If incompetence was to be expected, what actually happened was far worse. Had they cared to, the ex-clerks could have learned how to run the state monopolies. The state services were a mess, but there was nothing incompetent about the methods used by government officials to exploit their position. Price and currency regulations, impossible to enforce, pushed the elite toward greater corruption and smuggling. The Guinean Franc was of little value outside the country. So officials built luxurious villas in Conakry and rented them for hard currency to foreign embassies; they then used the currency to buy luxury goods—a black Mercedes, for example. When surplus U.S. rice showed up in the markets of neighboring countries, it was obvious that the rice was not carried out of Guinea sack by sack on bush trails; it went over in trucks that passed the many police check points that dot the roads. When we crossed over to Sierra Leone, we heard of an odd case of corruption caused by the Guinean Franc. The district officer of Kambia in Sierra Leone told us of a recent plea from the Guinean commandant across the border. The commandant's car had needed repairs. He could not get the necessary parts in Guinea, so he took the car to a garage in Freetown, capital of Sierra Leone. Now he had to pay the garage bill of about forty pounds; the garage would not, of course, accept Guinean Francs. So he asked the district officer if he could sell enough peanuts in the Kambia market to raise the sterling he needed to pay the bill. The district officer did not know where the commandant got the peanuts; it seemed clear, though, that he did not grow them himself.

Sékou Touré's attitude toward the rampant corruption around him is ambivalent. He often denounces dishonesty in his radio broadcasts, and the general opinion is that he is personally incorruptible. On his tours upcountry, he often fires or jails officials found guilty of corruption or brutality. Early in 1963, several months after a major scandal in the national bank, Touré abruptly announced that all currency was to be exchanged for new bills; his aim was to uncover those who were holding suspiciously large amounts of money. But Touré's financial punch was telegraphed: more than a month before it happened, I was told, in a casual conversation, that Touré had had the currency "secretly" printed in Britain. (The first Guinean Francs were printed in Czechoslovakia.) But though Touré is tough on minor officials, he seems to do nothing about the corruption of those closest to him, though it is glaringly obvious in their villas and their Mercedes. Similarly with the diversion of Guinea's resources and foreign aid to prestige projects. Touré could have prevented much of the waste—he could certainly have told the commandant of N'Zérékoré not to build him a villa—but he did not.

Touré himself is a member of the elite, despite his frequent criticisms of it. He has written movingly of the alienation of the educated Africans from their own people, and as he says himself, he too is alienated. So the psychological needs of the African elite, imposed by the experiences of their generation, are partly the needs of Sékou Touré, even though in another context he will recognize these needs for what they are. This duality in Touré, which exists in so many Africans, appeared in his radio report to the nation on February 25, 1962. At one point he gave priority to agriculture in economic planning, while admitting that the plan was "behind schedule." Later, when he listed necessary government investments that are "noneconomic," he put "the expenses of sovereignty, such as embassies," at the head of the list.

As for the great hope of Guinea, human investment, it was sadly obvious by late 1962 that it too was a failure. In February 1962, the party newspaper, *Horoya,* made great claims on its behalf: in the three preceding years, according to *Horoya*'s figures, 1,648 schools and about two thousand other buildings were put up by human investment. But already Guinea was de-emphasizing human investment. Touré and other leaders called it a technique of "regional utility"; in my conversations with Guinean officials, human investment was not discussed unless I brought it up. It clearly was no longer an important part of Guinean political mythology. In view of this, the figures given by *Horoya* are undoubtedly exaggerated, if not fabricated. If they were accurate, Guinea would have reason indeed to boast about the results of human investment; yet, at the five-day party congress held in December 1962, human investment was never mentioned. It almost seemed as if it had never existed.

The reasons for the failure of human investment are complex. In essence, though, the conditions for its success were not met: the projects were not felt by the people to be of use to them; the people did not participate in choosing the projects; there was no clear assignment of responsibilities between the people and the state (for maintenance of roads, for example); neither state nor people could hold the other to performance of their responsibilities.

Human investment started in 1959 with a burst of enthusiasm, and 752 building projects were completed, according to the government, in the first year. At first, it seems, the people were willing to participate, especially since in many cases human investment consisted of one or two skilled men working while the rest of the village danced—there is a limit to the use of unskilled hands in construction. But many of the early projects quickly disintegrated: roads disappeared, buildings fell apart, because they were badly built or unneeded or no one was held responsible for their maintenance.

Soon officials began using human investment for their own ends. As Victor D. DuBois of the American Universities Field Staff has pointed out, there was a great shift in emphasis after the first year. In 1959, human investment was credited with building 134 headquarters, administrative office buildings and administrators' houses. But in 1960 the figure rose to 616, and in 1961 to 1043. More and more, then, human investment was directed to the desires and comforts of the elite, not to the needs of the people. More and more, it resembled the forced labor imposed by the French a generation before. Ugly reports circulated of brutal methods used by officials to get the people to work, and workers' brigades were put to tilling fields for officials—perhaps growing peanuts for sale in Sierra Leone. Popular resistance grew, and gradually the PDG gave up human investment. It might have continued it by using Stalinist tactics, but that sort of officially organized brutality is alien to Guinea, as it is to most of Africa.

The collapse of human investment illustrates the basic failure of the PDG: it did not succeed in giving political power to the people. Despite the party's theories, it was the elite that ruled, uncontrolled. The harness Touré had fashioned for the elite—the party machinery—had no noticeable restraining effect. So the elite spent the country's resources for its own ends and abused the ideal of human investment; it is particularly ironic that the people were forced to build headquarters for the party that in theory was to give them power over the very men who were dragooning them.

As with *animation rurale,* the record of what actually happened within the party is buried in hundreds of obscure struggles in distant villages. It is impossible to say to what extent the elite withheld power from the people (officials using their power to crush efforts by the local party to control them), and to what extent the people failed to use the channels theoretically open to them. All the outward symbols of power and prestige—buildings, uniforms, cars, guns—were with the elite officials as they had been with the French; a party statute written in Conakry was not enough, under the best of circumstances, to convince a local party committee made up of illiterate peasants that they could overrule the commandant, prime symbol of authority under colonial rule. As Touré has often complained, the Guinean who took over from a Frenchman as commandant frequently adopted the Frenchman's behavior as well as his uniform.

On this issue, Torré is not at all ambiguous. In speech after speech, he calls on the people to watch over the administration and castigates officials who exceed their powers. Here is what Touré was saying in his broadcasts of early 1962:

> The democratic principle is the one that is most neglected. . . . Some regions . . . substitute for democratic practices authoritarian methods which create absurd conflicts between the administrative and political authorities . . . and repel the party members.
>
> The continuing faults [in the administration] are doubtless due to the political, intellectual and moral incapacity of some of our cadres. . . .
>
> The refusal, often observed on the part of administrators, to establish intimate cooperation . . . with the political leaders is due to their unacceptable lack of confidence in the political capacities of

the representatives of the people, or sometimes even to an intolerable contempt for the masses. . . .

If the pre-eminence of the party had been honestly affirmed, we would not have seen the abuses of authority committed by some dishonest or incapable officials. And, wherever these abuses have occurred, the people live in coercion and fear. It is our [party] sections that are responsible for these facts.

After one of his inspection tours, during which he jailed a number of officials and annulled forced marriages, Touré asked: "Why is it that what is possible during an inspection tour is not possible during the regional [party] conferences? It is because the leaders of local party committees generally restrict freedom of expression . . . and try constantly to escape the supervision of the party membership. But if debate is avoided, the problems remain and accumulate." On an earlier occasion, Touré advised the people: "You must maintain surveillance over everyone, beginning with President Sékou Touré. If you are a laborer or a farmer, say to yourself that you are the equal of Monsieur Touré, above any minister, above any public servant. . . ."

But there is no evidence yet that the people believe they are "above any public servant," and the party itself does not respond to Touré's urging. The PDG has not succeeded in "animating" the elite, or in "decolonizing" its behavior. Because of this failure, the elite remains a massive barrier to putting the party's theory into practice. In December 1962, the elite in effect defeated Touré at the party congress at which the Bureau Politique National came up for re-election. Before the election, Touré let it be known that, with a greater supply of educated Guineans now available, the party might drop those members of the BPN who were corrupt or incompetent. The suggestion was ignored: all seventeen members of the BPN were re-elected. Observers at the congress spoke of *"immobilisme"* in the party; after five years, the men in power seemed more interested in protecting their positions than in revolutionizing their society. Touré, whose rule is by no means absolute, did not try to overturn the congress' decision. He shifted the center of power from the BPN to the government, and in so doing violated his own principle of party supremacy.

The evidence, then, is plentiful for a pessimistic view of Guinea. In 1962 the air of discouragement was obvious; by 1964 it seemed, if anything, worse. After four feverish years, so much in the Guinean mythology had proved to be illusion: the Plan and human investment had failed, the vaunted agricultural cooperatives were (their director said to me) "largely fantasies." Little if any effort was being made to get the long, difficult and complex process of developing agriculture under way. The PDG had built a machine through which it could reach the people, but in this Thermidor of the Guinean Revolution the party had nothing very fresh to say. It had exhorted the people for four years; in retrospect it could be seen that what the party was doing was simply cheerleading—it did not offer much of direct value to the people. Touré was acutely aware of this. On February 18, 1962, he said: "If we are running into failures in the execution of the plan . . . these will without any doubt affect the ultimate course of the national revolution. Endlessly repeating slogans, parading ideas, approving principles: these do not make a revolution." And a week later: "The people have put their trust in the party to lead them to promised objectives . . . but if [the people] come to believe that there is a contradiction between what the party proclaims and what is being done, distrust will certainly grow, and you will agree that it is easier to get the people's confidence than to regain it [once it is lost]." The basic barrier in Guinea is the same as that in Senegal: the elite's opposition to social change. The idea of democracy within the party, bridging the gap between the state and the people, is obviously distasteful to the elite. So, although Touré is known as a "radical" and Senghor as a "conservative," their speeches are indistinguishable when they are talking about the elite.

The optimists' case for Guinea is much less tangible; it rests on an insubstantial web of impressions and possibilities. In our travels through the interior of Guinea, we sensed a fresh breeze blowing: it was, we felt, the most *African,* the most decolonized, country we had been in. Everywhere in Africa we were greeted with hospitality, but our acceptance in Guinea seemed untainted by Uncle Tomism toward bearers of European culture. Discouragement seemed to have bred a healthy realism among many officials. Two examples stand out among many. Camara Daouda, permanent secretary of the BPN, discussed the problem of the elite with pragmatic frankness unclouded by ideology. In the remote town of Beyla, two local officials admitted good-humoredly that nothing had been done, but said that the climate was beginning to change. One said: "We have to produce now—no more dancing." The other added: "We pushed the people around before, now the people are beginning to push us."

The people are not pushing on any great scale, or in any visible directions. Their successful resistance to the abuses of human investment was purely negative; whether they are becoming any readier to accept useful new ideas remains unknown, but it may be that the PDG's actions in the past five years have begun to unleash popular energies. It is impossible to measure the effect on African women of the new role in which they are theoretically cast, yet this may be the key to Guinea's future. If the exploited Guinean women demand a more productive society—if they are truly "animated"—this may prove to be far more important than all the failures of the last five years.

The ambiguities of Guinea are endless. A characteristically African pragmatism and humor coexists peacefully with the party's theoretical rigidity and the Emperor Jones behavior of the elite. Never was this more clear than during the tour that Félix Houphouet-Boigny, President of the Ivory Coast, made in Guinea in October 1962. The tour was to seal the reconciliation of Houphouet and Touré, old allies who had split in 1958 when Houphouet went along with de Gaulle while Touré defied him. The effort that Guinea put into welcoming Houphouet was unbelievable; the government was virtually closed down for several weeks. Upcountry we saw men building dozens of triumphal arches across the road Houphouet was to travel; we were almost prevented from leaving the town of Labé because officials were trying to keep all vehicles on hand for Houphouet's welcome. On the road to Conakry, villagers were painting the houses that fronted on the highway. These were truly Potemkin villages: most houses were painted only on the front, a few on the sides, none on the rear. In N'Zérékoré and apparently some other towns, the opening of school was delayed for two weeks because the teachers' housing had been commandeered for the

Houphouet party, which spent exactly one night in N'Zérékoré. The party forced the people to buy new clothing for the welcoming parades. Members of the eighty-member Houphouet party told us they received from a hundred to five hundred dollars for pocket money at the border, and that their rooms each evening were stocked with whiskey, cigarettes and phonograph records. The commandants of the regions through which the tour passed were said to have each received $100,000 to get things ready. The cost to Guinea of putting on the dog for Houphouet was staggering. Estimates of the cash outlay ranged from two to eight million dollars. In addition, of course, the government was distracted from practically all other activities, and thousands of man-hours were spent to build those arches, to paint those villages (some were painted with whitewash that ran with the first rain).

One gala evening in Conakry, a play was put on for the visitors and the diplomatic colony. The play was in curious and refreshing contrast to the Houphouet tour. It was officially blessed—the play, written by party members in the town of Mamou, had been chosen over those of the rest of the country in an annual competition staged by the PDG. It was, as might be expected in revolutionary Guinea, a morality play about a typically African problem: the exodus of young men to the city. What might not be expected is that this morality play was done in slapstick and that it contained a merciless parody of the Guinean elite.

The play begins with two young men in a village who have been told by their girls that they will not marry them unless the boys go to the city and make some money. The young men say: "Never will we till the soil, never will we join the cooperative"—the litany of the

young African who has been to school. They decide to
go to Conakry. They ask the local marabout for magic
charms, promising to pay him on their return. No magic
on credit, says the marabout, and the boys dig up the
cash they claimed not to have. They trek to Conakry,
stopping occasionally to offer a slapstick prayer to the
"grande ville." The next scene opens in the home of a
government official who is distantly related to one of the
youths. The official, vastly self-important, is reading
Horoya, the party newspaper, and listening to the inevitable transistor radio; his wife is badgering him
about money, saying that they have no cash because
"Monsieur" insists on supporting hordes of relatives.
The official eases his feelings by ferociously chasing a
tattered and frightened servant around the room. When
the two youths arrive, one explains that he is Mamadou,
son of the official's cousin. "All my cousins have sons
named Mamadou," grunts the official, but eventually
the relation is established. The wife refuses to take them
in, and the official sends the boys away after he discovers
they have neither jobs nor party cards. The boys end up
as "wally-wallys," the ragged men who hang around the
port in the hope of odd jobs. Things get worse and
worse. Mamadou broods: "Once I had a name, Mamadou the Fortunate . . . Now I'm only Mamadou Wally-
Wally." Eventually, of course, they go back to the village, admit the error of their ways and all ends well with
their reacceptance by the village.

What is extraordinary in the play is the devastating
portrayal of the government official—a satire aimed
straight at the African members of the audience. Deliberately so, one of the authors told us later in Mamou.
"We gave it to everybody," he said cheerfully. The pretensions mocked by the play were the very pretensions

so vividly in evidence during the Houphouet tour. Yet no one seemed to mind. We saw Sékou Touré laughing uproariously down in the front row.

It is hard to imagine such a play being put on in the early years of, say, the Russian Revolution. This capacity for self-mockery helps protect Guinea from the solemn excesses of revolutionary fervor and may, perhaps, hasten the day when the elite begins to live up to its professed ideals. It is part of the slim body of evidence that justifies optimism about Guinea's future.

CHAPTER EIGHT

Education and
Rural Exodus

O F ALL THE MYTHS that afflict Africa today, the idea that education is a universal panacea is perhaps the most pernicious. More schools mean more development, many assume, and it seems a self-evident truth that education is a Good Thing. But progress in Africa involves radical change and, as Adam Curle wrote, "in most societies for most of recorded time, education has been a reactionary force rather than a progressive one." Whether education is useful depends on the values that are taught as well as the curriculum. Education in the traditional village society, the "bush school" that adolescents attended, was clearly not a progressive force, but a conservative one, since it taught rigid conformity. But the traditional school is losing ground, and the European-style school introduced by the colonial rulers is spreading rapidly; this is the training ground of the elite. The question, then, is whether this school serves Africa's needs. As we have seen repeatedly, progress in rural Africa is held up by two bottlenecks: lack of real communication between rural Africans and the ruling elite, and lack of innovating attitudes among farmers and the elite. The evidence indicates that the "modern" school does not help solve either problem, and that it may actually do more harm than good.

As in colonial times, the school today is a force that divides rather than unites. Since it has no contact with traditional African society, the school cuts its pupils off from their own community, creating those "deep divisions among us" that Sékou Touré called one of the consequences of European-style education. The alienation of the educated African was Europe's legacy, and the school is still teaching the same message; it cannot be otherwise, since the elite that provides the teachers was educated in those same schools. That message is, as it was under the Europeans, the superiority of all that is European-urban over what is African-rural. Contempt for village culture and its values, and above all contempt for farming and manual labor, is the lesson instilled in the students. Symbolically, it is common for schools to be built in European style, with imported materials, instead of using local materials and techniques. In the Ivory Coast, school boys grow long fingernails to prove they do not work with their hands (just as aristocratic Fulani women wear a complex hairdo to show they do not carry burdens); unfortunately, the school boys seldom work with their heads either.

In one little primary school, I saw on the wall a poster (printed, naturally, in Europe) that set out the school's teachings with hideous clarity. The poster showed two family groups. One was seated around a table, eating from plates with knives and forks; this group wore European clothes and lived in a European-style house, shown in the background. The other family group was squatting around the large bowl from which rural Africans eat with their hands. The parents wore African clothes, the kids were naked, and they lived in a thatched hut, also shown in the background. More clearly than a thousand words, this tattered poster drove home the poisonous message of the school: one family group was good—modern, the other bad—traditional. Yet there was no trace of evidence, in the scene the poster pictured, that the "modern" family was in fact "modern" in any but a superficial sense: nothing indicated that they were more productive, more sanitary, more educated (in any true sense) than the "traditional" family. Their "European" home is probably hotter than the thatched hut, and is beyond the means of most Africans; their clothes are more expensive and less comfortable. The poster was defining "modern" with a set of empty symbols: a building, a table, clothes, knife and fork. The children in the school were taught, then, that these outward symbols were what mattered: European dress before a more productive farm; eating at a table takes precedence over eating more protein. After this devastating lesson, it is no surprise that educated Africans so often adopt the form of Europe without the substance—the consumption without the production, the table without the protein. The culture the school taught was mock-European, not real European. And, of course, the rural African who has graduated from this primary school is virtually driven out of the village by the school's teaching that the ways of his domineering parents are primitive. By alienating its students, by teaching them contempt for village life, the European school makes it virtually impossible for the elite it produces to communicate with the farmers.

But alienation is the price of progress, it is argued. Traditional culture has to give way to the new; nobody believes in Noble Savages any more. The machines are coming, and Africans must be torn from the breast of their maternal civilization. It is painful, but it has to happen. The trouble with this reasoning is that it assumes that the European school is teaching Africans to be problem-solving Western types. But in fact the European school in Africa is just as conformist as the bush school, though it teaches a different conformity. As we saw in Chapter Two, the colonial school discouraged creativity. So does today's school. In most African schools, the curriculum still has little relevance to Africa's needs. The method of teaching is still rigid memorization; the purpose of schooling is to pass an examination that gets you into the elite, not to learn a subject which has little apparent relevance to your life. In its empty ritual, the European school resembles Koranic education, in which African children memorize large chunks of the Koran in Arabic, a language they do not understand. They do not learn the teachings of the Koran, but they do absorb a quite different lesson: the way to get ahead is to memorize a string of meaningless syllables. Much the same sort of teaching was found by Dr. Anne Colot, a French psychologist, in her 1963 study of the *cours d'initiation* (kindergarten) in Dakar. She observed the teaching of *morale* (roughly, "citizenship"). The children in one class were reciting this lesson in French: *"Avant de traverser la rue je regarde bien si une voiture ne vient pas."* ("Before crossing the street I look carefully to see if a car is coming.") Fifteen children recited the lesson in French without error. Then Dr. Colot asked each of these children in their own language, Wolof, the meaning of two simple key words in the sentence: *avant* ("before") and *si* ("if"). Of the fifteen pupils, none knew the meaning of *avant*

162

and only two knew the meaning of *si*. Without these two words the lesson had no ostensible meaning to the children who had so accurately committed it to memory. They did not learn how to jaywalk in the heavy traffic of Dakar. But they did learn how to please authority.

The results of this sort of teaching begin to show in secondary school, where foreign teachers complain that their African pupils are excellent at memorization but seem to have no interest in the subject matter of their studies. Later in life we find the fruit of these school attitudes in the African elite: the concern with status rather than production, the rigid application of rules without concern for their purpose and, worst of all, fear and dislike of anything new and risky. Take, for example, the Foyers Féminins in the Ivory Coast to which women go, ostensibly to learn reading, hygiene, sewing and so forth. It is common for the Ivorian woman teacher to make her pupils recite "We must filter our drinking water," and then drink unfiltered water herself from the tap while the class watches. Senseless? Not entirely, it seems to me, for, once again, the true purpose of the lesson is the lesson itself: to recite the European phrase, with its illusion of modernity, rather than actually to filter the water.

Here, in the school, is the cause of many of the rural fiascos described in earlier chapters. So far as farming is concerned, not caring or knowing *how* to use knowledge and reason leads only to waste: it is of no value for the extension agent to know that these fields can benefit from fertilizer, unless he also cares enough to make the effort to find out if this particular fertilizer really works, to convince the villagers that they should use it, and to make sure—perhaps by hounding other officials—that it is delivered to the village on time.

Rural schools also have a depressing effect on the entire village community. The young men they graduate should be the means of introducing change to the villages, for the older people are impervious to new ideas coming from outside their world. Only the young can make the village a place worth living in, for themselves and their children. Yet the European-style school methodically decapitates rural society by lopping off those who should be its natural leaders and sending them to stagnate in the cities. It was on the basis of these facts that the planning team of Louis-Joseph Lebret concluded that the present school system is a "negative" influence on development. These remarks, written about Senegal, are applicable generally to Africa, for the situation they describe grew out of the colonial experience:

> It seems, particularly in rural society, that no bridge exists between the two cultures ["traditional" and "modern"] and that the rural elites produced by schooling have a very slight influence on the evolution of traditional society.
>
> [For primary school graduates] the separation between the two cultures is complete, and their exodus is certain, first to the rural towns, then to the cities.

The growing migration of rural youth to the cities, one of Africa's most menacing social problems, is thus in part caused by the schools. Rural exodus is, of course, a familiar phenomenon all over the world—"how're you going to keep 'em down on the farm?" is not a question that was first asked in Africa. But the African youths are not going from farm to factory in the pattern familiar to Western nations. There is no factory to hire them.

Africa's exodus is not part of an industrial revolution, and the forces that drive the youth of Africa to the cities are only in part economic. Most of the young men are *leaving* the village, rather than *going* to the city. Their main interest is fleeing a traditional society in which the young are dominated by the old and a man starting out in agriculture has little hope of ever rising above the level of subsistence. His parents exploit him, and since he has little money for bride-price, he cannot compete against older men for the unmarried girls in the village: "the girl's heart belongs to the young man, but the old man owns her body." Life in the village is dull; there is little for him to do. Life in the city, as he dimly sees it from afar, is just the opposite. In the city he will be free of the heavy hand of the old people of the village; he will be able to find girls; he has heard of the high-paying jobs others have gotten in the capital; there are movies and automobiles and fine clothes there. Better transportation, the tales of returning travelers, and the transistor radio carry the lure of the city farther and farther into the bush.

The young graduate of primary school, already somewhat alienated from his parents, sets out for the city with slim intellectual baggage. He can read and write a European language, as a rule badly, and has a smattering of arithmetic and some general knowledge. For reasons ranging from protein deficiency through large classes (sixty or more is frequent) to the irrelevancy of the curriculum, the African youth has learned less than he could have in his six years of school, and he has not learned how, or why, to learn. The youth knows nothing of agriculture and has no trade to offer the city job market.

When he reaches the city, he will, if he is lucky, find

food and shelter with a relative. He will then look for work, with high hopes, since he knows of someone who made it with no more qualification than he. He haunts government offices, since the state is the largest and most desirable source of jobs.

But every day the odds against this young man grow longer. The equation is simple: stagnant African economics are producing few new jobs; governments overloaded with employees and running at a deficit cannot afford to add to the burden on their payrolls; the remaining Europeans hold highly skilled jobs for which the young man is not qualified; and with more schools being built, the supply of young men increases at an ever faster rate. Our young man is not likely, therefore, to find his ideal: a government clerkship. But he will usually refuse manual labor, and he will surely not go back to his village to farm. He is not qualified for any skilled or semiskilled manual trade, and its status is far too low for his expectations. Family solidarity—the obligation to support one's relations—allows him to live on in town indefinitely without working, and to be unemployed is far less humiliating than to work with his hands or, worst of all, to be a farmer.

The young man rots away in shantytown, that land of human waste that is part of every African capital. As the years go by, he forgets his little schooling—lapsed readers are common—and in time he is not only unemployed, he is unemployable. He may become passive and withdrawn; mental illness is common. He is bitter, for he senses that he has been betrayed. The school taught him that he belonged in the elite, but when he knocked at the gate he found there was no more room in the privileged class. Every day he sees, as he stands in shabby idleness on a street corner, the officials driving by in

their Mercedes, in their expensive suits, with their
pretty women. They are going to the airconditioned
villas; he has to go back to his hovel in shantytown.
Even if he finds a small clerkship, he is likely to be bitter
as he contemplates the yawning gap between his pay
and that of the upper ranks of the elite. That gap is far
greater in Africa than in the industrial nations, just as
the elite–peasant gap is far greater, for the men in the
upper ranks receive the pay and privilege of their European predecessors, while he, the clerk, is paid as were
the African auxiliaries. The gap was perhaps less painful
when it was just between Africans and foreigners, but
our young clerk knows that the man in the Mercedes
only yesterday was a clerk like himself.

The uprooted young men, exiles in their own land,
crossed our path many times in our years in Africa.
Their faces haunt the memory. They are the two youths
we took from the deep bush to Dakar, who spoke bit-
terly of peasants as "savages." They are the men who sell
you cigarettes or souvenirs in Lagos or Accra, the young
man who drifted over to the car and asked my wife for a
job ("Please, hire me as an apprentice?" "Apprentice
what?" "Apprentice anything!"), the bright youth in
Dahomey who offered to wash, drive or sell the car for
us. Their faces are bitter sometimes, anxious and ingra-
tiating; their dress is shabby but usually European.
They are, also, Mamadou Ka, who often stopped by our
little house in Dakar. Mamadou Ka was an unemployed
auto mechanic; at the age of about twenty-five, he had
been out of a job for more years than he had worked
since he left school in his mid-teens, without a degree.
He soon discovered there was nothing we could do to
help him find work, and he never asked us for anything.
Yet, every couple of days, Mamadou stopped in for an

167

hour's chat. Why? We never really knew. He showed no more than a mild curiosity about our foreign ways; but he had little else to do during the long idle days.

My wife taught a group of school dropouts for several months. These young men, mostly in their mid-twenties, had started secondary school, but dropped out, for one reason or another, before getting the "brevet" diploma. The "brevet," which is won by examination after a minimum of four years of secondary school, opens the doors of the elite class: with a brevet, a Senegalese is sure to be hired by the state. Some of my wife's students had jobs, most did not; all knew they would be safe if only they could pass the brevet. The small Centre de Bopp, where she taught, had organized night classes in each of the subjects on which brevet candidates are examined. My wife taught English; and it is a mark of the insanity of the school system that these young men, already having trouble enough with French (perhaps their *fourth* language), should be forced to learn a second, and utterly irrelevant, European language. (In Conakry, German is taught in the *lycée!*) Sometimes in the evenings we sat around and chatted with the brevet students. Their conversation centered on criticism of the elite in power and the problems of young men; young women, for instance. One youth had made an agreement with a girl's father to pay the bride-price over a year, giving over each month a substantial part of his salary. Late in the year, the parents found a wealthier match and canceled the engagement without returning any of his money . . . What struck us about my wife's students was the sterile and negative tone to their criticism. Though they were more enterprising than most of their fellows—since they were still trying to get the brevet (though most of them failed)—they did not seem to have

168

any productive ideas for their lives. They were bitter at the elite for closing the gate in their faces, but they did not reject the elite system itself. If one day they were to storm the palace, we sensed, their revolution would be destructive rather than creative.

The schools that produce these dangerous young men are being multiplied all over Africa by governments convinced that "modernization" can be measured by the rate of literacy. Already some African states are educationally overdeveloped—by comparison to Europe at a similar stage of economic growth—and yet the flood has just begun. At present a secondary school graduate in most places is assured of a job, but as the flow increases, the level of educated unemployment will rise with it. In Madagascar, as early as 1962, the Planning Commission said thirty thousand new jobs a year were needed to take care of youths with the brevet or a higher degree, but that it seemed unlikely the economy would produce more than two or three thousand new jobs for at least five years. In time, if the present trend continues, unemployment will reach the university graduates.

Since there are far fewer secondary than primary schools, most primary school graduates are unable to go on. In testimony to the irrelevant nature of education, the dropout rate is fantastically high at all levels: usually a majority of those who start primary school fail to graduate, and a majority of those who go on do not finish secondary school. These are the school-leavers who are providing the present flood into the cities. The crest of the wave is being formed for the future in hundreds of new schools, but the volume already is appalling: Nigeria alone expects soon to have 650,000 unemployed school dropouts. In this young continent—half the African population is under twenty years old—the potential flood of young men is beyond any conceivable hope for new jobs to satisfy them.

If the young men's calculations were based on money alone, it might, at least in theory, be possible to settle them on the land. But their refusal to farm is based more on considerations of status than earnings. Dahomey, a country where the rural exodus is particularly acute, found this out with a project for which official hopes were high. Thirty school-leavers, all volunteers, were settled at a place called Hinvi; the state cleared the land, built dormitories, and started the young men off growing cotton. Six months later, after selling their crop and paying back state advances, each youth netted forty dollars. (The average peasant earns less than thirty dollars in a year.) The young men were given a two-week vacation, at their request. Only one-third of them returned to Hinvi from the vacation. Pressure on relatives netted another third, but ten never came back. That forty dollars was more than any, or almost any, of the young men had ever earned—still, a majority of them did not want to go on working at Hinvi. For staying in Hinvi as farmers would have been an admission of defeat, a renunciation of the dreams instilled in them by the school they attended. They would have been stranded on the "primitive" peasant shore of their divided society. In the city there is always hope, no matter how dim. In poker terms, the young men who quit Hinvi were splitting a pair of sixes to draw to a straight.

Nigeria's Western Region has also found the economics of settling school-leavers on the land to be forbidding. Each year about fifty thousand new dropouts join the ranks of the urban unemployed in the Region. In 1963 a government report on earlier settlement schemes estimated their cost at almost twelve thousand dollars per settler. At this rate, the settling of ten thousand school-leavers—only one-fifth of the annual crop of dropouts—would cost the equivalent of 44 per cent of the Western Region's development budget! It would cost *twice* the entire development budget to settle just the new school-leavers, and it would be depressingly certain that many of them would flee the land at the first opportunity. It is hardly surprising, then, that the Western Region decided that settling the school-leavers was "too expensive."

Too expensive it certainly is, and the Nigerian calculation does not begin to measure the true price. Other costs must be added in the total bill. First, of course, is the cost of schooling the young men so they come to the city and need to be resettled. The cost in sheer human waste is incalculable. The young men drifting idly in the cities, their souls eaten away gradually by the acids of failure, are not producing for the African economy. They are not growing food on the land, not making goods in a factory. Africa's young men, like youth anywhere, should provide the strong productive arms on which the economy rests. Instead, this youth is being wasted, and the young men are still more parasites on a peasantry already afflicted with too many parasites.

Is this "education for development"—or is it, rather, economic lunacy? It is, of course, lunacy for Africa to pay the price it does—in bitter wasted youth, in education budgets—for schools if they actually retard its development. Yet the governments go on putting up schools at a breakneck pace; the very states, like Western Nigeria and Dahomey, that are struggling unsuccessfully with their present school-leavers are building schools to ensure that the problem will increase rather than diminish. In the normal terms of political analysis, this looks incredible, since the elite seems to be cutting its own throat, and that of the economy.

If the elite goes on devoting its scarce resources to a school system that poisons the society and threatens the elite's own position, it is because Africa's rulers are prisoners of the myth of education. Only an idea with the force of myth could survive the imposing logic that argues against Africa's schools. If the issue were between, say, two forms of fertilizer, the Africans, and even their foreign advisers, doubtless would make the choice dictated by logic. But education is so obviously "good" that rational decision is impossible. Perhaps the schools could be improved, it is often conceded, but the idea that they are on balance harmful is rejected as somehow out of bounds and eccentric. (The tyranny of words: if the word "indoctrination" were substituted for "education" throughout this chapter, the ideas expressed might seem far less radical.) Westerners tend to assume because our systems of education teach us to be creative types—in technical if not in social fields—that it will do the same for the Africans. The lesson of agriculture—that you cannot easily transplant technology from one environment to another—applies to education as well. The seed that grows in Iowa will not grow in the tropical soil of the Congo; the educational technology that works in Europe does not function in the different culture of Africa. I am not arguing, of course, that Africa should dispense with education. To reverse the example used earlier of the agricultural extension agent, it is not enough for him to want to introduce fertilizer to the village unless he has the technical knowledge needed to apply and test the fertilizer. And even an unmotivated technician may do a certain amount of good; a careless doctor is perhaps better than no doctor at all. But many of the new methods needed by rural Africa are relatively simple and easily mastered by anyone who has the desire. Though both are needed, motivation is more essential, and difficult to ensure, than technical skill. As long as education has the effects it does today, Africa will continue to pay a dreadfully high price for what benefits it gets from its schools.

Criticism of education is not accepted easily by Africans. Past experience leads them to suspect any argument based on the idea that African schools should be different from European schools. That is "second-rate" education, they say, because the Europeans believe that Africans are inferior, and hope to keep the Africans inferior by preventing them from eating the fruit of the Tree of Knowledge. In nations once under British rule, the Africans have bitter memories of the schools run by missionaries, who taught their black pupils to keep their (inferior) place in a white-ruled world. Against the emotionally charged background of colonial attitudes, it is only natural that when Africans hear "different" they think "inferior," and that they insist on copies of schools designed for another culture in another era.

Some small improvements have been made since independence. The texts have been rewritten so that they no longer give an exclusively European (*"nos ancêtres les gaulois"*) view of history. Many nations are spreading out their secondary schools, so that students are not automatically brought to the capital. Guinea requires that postprimary students go out of their own ethnic area, a useful technique for stimulating national rather than tribal loyalties. Everywhere there is some effort to stress technical over classical education. Some nations—Mali and Dahomey are examples—have plans for a sweeping reorganization of primary schooling: most students would get a practical agricultural education, with just enough conventional study to be literate and do arithmetic; a minority would be sent on to elite schools. But so far these plans exist mainly on paper, and interest in actually applying them seems minimal.

None of these reforms is the kind of surgical operation that African education needs. The schools, after all, can hardly do more than reflect the values of the rulers of the society. If the schools divide Africans instead of uniting them, this is the natural result of the agonizing gap between the village and the elite. The Europeans succeeded all too well. When men like Kwame Nkrumah and Sékou Touré write of the alienation produced by European education, they write in the first person, for they too, like all the elite, are permanently scarred by their experience. What the schools teach is what the elite believes: the teacher himself at heart believes the message of that poster that defines "modern" as an "imitation European"; nor does he seem to care that his class memorizes without learning, for that is what he did. For this reason, there is not much drive within the elite to remake the schools. When in November 1962 representatives of twenty African nations gathered in Cotonou to discuss rural exodus, their final resolution did not include among its thirty-two demands any reference to school reform. Any real change in education must wait on a change in values. The creation of a school system that aids rather than hinders creativity, that unites instead of alienating its pupils, can come only after Africa has accomplished its spiritual decolonization, after it has found its new identity, its own set of values.

The time may be short, for every day the dangerous young men flow into the city. Clustered in shantytowns in the margin of society, they wait and hope. As their chances decrease, hope dims, bitterness grows, and the city becomes a tinderbox of revolution.

Pierre Biarnés, the editor of *Le Moniteur Africain,* contends that even if African development plans were carried out in full—which will not happen, as we have seen—the new jobs created would not come close to satisfying the demand. Biarnés asks:

> Then what? How to dam the flood of new generations of "intellectuals" without jobs or holding jobs they consider inferior? How to prevent the upsetting of the political structure that will almost certainly be caused by the substitution for the present rulers of a new class steeped in bitterness? And backed by a populace that is no less bitter? All these guests invited to a party where there are not enough seats?

CHAPTER NINE

Foreign Aid:
The New Missionaries

T HE END of colonial rule did not end foreign influence in Africa, it only changed some of its forms. As
means of communication improve, the impact of the
industrial nations, in goods and ideas alike, continues to
grow. Politics, like nature, abhors a vacuum; the apparent power vacuum in the new African states has sucked
most of the richer countries into what Julius Nyerere of
Tanganyika calls the "second scramble for Africa." An
African capital nowadays is an incredible tower of Babel
in which a dozen discordant voices are telling the Africans, in essence, "Be like *us*," and offering money in return for the privilege of fashioning Africa in the for-
eigner's image.

The techniques of aid vary, from the grandiose spending of the French to the modest investment of the
Israelis, but they have in common their corrupting effect
on the African elites. Some of the corruption is overt:
many of the showpieces being put up around Africa are
financed by foreigners. Houphouet-Boigny's palace in

Abidjan was paid for by France, and the East Germans built the Imprimerie Patrice Lumumba in Conakry.

Corruption takes subtler forms than palaces. In their insistence, backed by money and power, that the Africans must imitate them, the foreigners are encouraging the elites not to rely on themselves, but on foreigners. By rejecting, usually without even considering the question, the idea of African solutions to African problems, they push the Africans, all too successfully, to believe that it is only a question of *whom* to imitate. The true liberation of Africa, the liberation of African souls to seek their own identity, is only postponed. This is true even in a literal sense. By replacing African effort, foreign aid has the effect of prolonging Africa's economic dependence on the outside world—the evidence is clear in the growing trade deficits of most African nations. Aid distorts economic calculations. Foreign exchange should be the most precious kind of money, since it is the hardest to earn, but since aid makes it "free," Africans are encouraged to import what they could and should produce themselves. A Guinean official, discussing a Yugoslav water project, commented frankly: "I'd never agree to it if it were our money—the job could be done for half what it will cost them."

The endless flow of foreign money shields the elite from the consequences of their wasteful habits and encourages "client–state" attitudes (familiar to the U.S. from its experiences with such nations as Laos and South Vietnam). As long as the money keeps coming in, there is no real reason to balance the budget, or at least use the deficit for development instead of waste—who among us treats other people's money like his own? Subtly, Africans come to accept the idea that foreigners know best—Guinea asked the Peace Corps to send cooperative organizers to the bush, though this job above all is one that should be done by Africans.

In their different ways, France and Soviet Russia have seemed to be the worst offenders. France under de Gaulle has maintained a political and military stake in Black Africa unmatched in 1964 by any other foreign power. Financing this presence cost the French government about half a billion dollars a year (though a good part of this amount comes back to France in trade, shipping, construction and salaries to Frenchmen in Africa). About eight thousand Frenchmen were working for African governments in 1964, half of them as teachers. France kept its African clients tied to it in many ways. Their trade was tied to the French market under complex deals in which France pays above the market price for African produce and in return sells its goods to Africa at artificial prices. French troops are still stationed in Africa, and under the usual treaty between de Gaulle and his clients, the African governments can call on France for military support, as Gabon's regime did in 1964. Despite the intervention in Gabon, it was clear by 1964 that France was interested in reducing its massive presence in Africa. De Gaulle began withdrawing troops and reducing his aid. Like the other great powers, France was finding that the client–state system does not always work. It costs too much for its economic and political rewards. When several patrons are available, no one of them can keep a real leash on even his weakest clients, for they can always switch to another patron. This was demonstrated in 1964 when the Central African Republic, one of the weakest of France's ex-colonies, began what seemed to be a switch from dependence on France to Communist China. The flow of French financial aid, though diminishing, has been massive and undermining to the African nations' independence. The poorer nations, such as Dahomey, depended on France until recently for part of their regular budget, as well as virtually all their development money. Little of France's spending has gone to productive projects. Most has gone into either showpieces or "social" investment, like schools and hospitals, that saddle the African government with continuing costs that it cannot afford. As a result, the African economies are peculiarly distorted: they have an "overhead" in social services that their economies cannot finance. Where foreign spending is particularly heavy, it actually reduces the standard of living. In Abidjan, capital of the Ivory Coast, a favorite French ally, the cost of living is said to have risen till it was the second most expensive capital in the world (after Caracas, Venezuela), while wages remained practically stationary.

The Russians in Africa have behaved like early capitalists, and clumsy capitalists at that. Their most spectacular effort was in Guinea, where they rushed in after independence in 1958. They tied Guinea up in trade deals that mortgaged the nation's exports to pay for Russian aid, but that aid did nothing to help Guinea produce enough to pay off the debts. As we saw in Chapter Seven, the Russians concentrated on elite-pleasing showpieces. Only the consumer goods sent by the Communist bloc could have succeeded in making the colonial trading companies look good by comparison. These companies, Unilever and the French CFAO and others, gouged their customers mercilessly, as we had the chance to observe every time we bought their imports in other African countries. Their prices would make S.S. Pierce blush, but when we arrived in Guinea late in 1962, we found that the Russians made the colonial traders look like Macy's. If the colonial companies gouged the African consumers, the Russians insulted them. Their goods were shoddy, incredibly overpriced and sometimes wildly inappropriate to Guinea. In one small store in Conakry, we noticed a can of Russian pineapple selling for a dollar; outside the store a Guinean woman was selling her country's pineapples, the most delicious we have ever tasted, at twenty-five cents a piece. Having heard that there was "nothing in the stores," we were surprised to see the vast store of canned goods and bottles in Nafaya, the main state store in Conakry. But on closer examination, we found that almost half the cans were—Bulgarian sesame paste! (I have no idea what the Bulgarians do with sesame paste. Neither, unfortunately, do the Guineans.) In Dakar, trading companies sell inferior wine at twice the price charged in France; but in Conakry, Eastern European wine, still poorer in quality, sells for four times the Dakar price. The famous Russian snowplows were, according to most authorities, including the United States Embassy, a myth that caught the fancy of the Western press; but the Communist powers *did* send such oddities as thousands of ladies' handbags, seats for nonexistent toilets, and agricultural machines with the exhaust piped through the cab—to keep the driver warm!

Much of the Russian performance must be attributed, not to evil Communist design, but to simple ignorance, incompetence and the general low quality of Soviet consumer goods. But not all of it. Sugar is a case in point. In Labé in the north of Guinea, we first encountered the celebrated unmelting Russian sugar, which resists the hottest coffee and is said to be able to tear the treads of automobile tires. (This of course is how the Russians want their sugar, since they hold it in their mouths and suck tea through it.) A few days after we first tasted (or tried to taste) the Russian variety, we went to a store in Conakry to buy sugar. When I saw the Russian script on the box, I asked the clerk if he didn't have sugar that would melt. He laughed and assured me that the sugar the Russians were now sending was "different." It was—it melted. Almost certainly what we bought was *Cuban* sugar, re-exported by the Russians and thereby depriving Cuba of one of its markets. In the same way, the Russians re-export the fruits they take from Guinea in barter; Eastern European nations are said to have complained at the quantities of fruit the Russians have forced them to take.

One senses, in the Russian policy in Guinea, that someone in Moscow has read a textbook on imperialist economic policy. Their trade deals—tying Guinea into a system of artificial prices and barter that makes it hard for her to trade elsewhere—are uncannily like the French *pacte colonial*. Like the French, the Russians offer a higher price for Guinea's exports and then charge more for their own goods. Our imaginary Soviet textbook probably also explains how the early imperialists sold baubles to African rulers, got them into debt and thereby gained control of them. Accordingly, the Russians sold Guinea tanks and useless goods and fancy buildings, all on credit; Guinea's inability to pay off her debts should then have made it possible for the Russians to hold her on a short leash. But the textbook apparently did not go on to say that the rules of the colonial game have been changed, in part by the Russians themselves. As the French have discovered, the essence of the cold war in Africa is that debts are meaningless now that the industrial powers are competing among themselves. The Guineans proved they understood this in November 1961 when Sékou Touré ousted the Soviet ambassador. What did it matter that Guinea owed Russia thirty-five million dollars or so—as long as the United States Embassy was just down the street?

The United States aid effort in Africa is refreshingly free of the most obvious corrupting aspects of French and Soviet aid. Probably this is because the U.S. is not as deeply involved in any one country—though Guinea and even Nigeria, the darling of the West, may one day become American client–states. The U.S. has been far less free with military aid than the other two powers; in 1963 the Americans let the Russians outbid them for the privilege of giving Somalia the equipment for a crushingly expensive army. The U.S. has engaged in some spectaculars for the elite—jet planes for Ethiopia and unneeded universities for Nigeria—but it is less guilty than France and Russia. American surplus food probably has a depressing effect on African food production, but at least the food is eaten by people who need it.

The Peace Corps may be a rare case of aid to Africa that serves a useful purpose. The Peace Corps and the private Operation Crossroads-Africa offer an image of "Europeans" that is in direct contrast to the somnolent, feudal colonial administrator of the past, Africa's previous example of what is "modern." Though they are well-educated and, being Americans, obviously rich, these young people work with their hands as the Europeans never did, live modestly and are more truly democratic than the Europeans or the African elites themselves. (A few other foreigners, notably Israelis, behave the same way. But they are rare.) Hopefully, they can help break down, at least a little bit, those elite attitudes that are so imposing a block to African development.

Operation Crossroads-Africa, which sends American

students to work on construction projects with African students during the summer vacation, clearly has this kind of impact on the Africans. In Dakar, Lamine Ba, a young Senegalese teacher, told me about his summer with Crossroads. Ba, an intelligent and emotional man, was concerned, far more than most Africans, with race prejudice in America. "I went with Crossroads to find out if Americans could be as bad as I had been told," he said. What Ba learned was not an answer to that question. His attitude toward American racism was not greatly changed, he was not overwhelmingly fond of the Americans he met, but—"The Americans worked while we Senegalese loafed. I was ashamed of some of our students. American girls worked harder than African men." Harold R. Isaacs, in his *Emergent Americans: A Report on Crossroads-Africa,* collected reactions from Nigerian students who worked with Americans. These were some of the Nigerians' impressions:

> I was exceedingly startled to find the great work that had been done by these young students within five and a half hours . . . there was the spirit of responsibility in them that we can never expect to find here. . . . I was forced to think about the shame we youths are likely [to inflict] on Nigeria. With only school certificates, we feel that manual work should be despised and relegated [out of] our lives. But here we are with University students who have traveled over nine thousand miles to do such work as we call base and mean here in Nigeria.
>
> I could see that they are not too big to do anything. . . . Imagine the road they are constructing; if it were us students, at least two or more students would have to be suspended or caned sev-

eral times or driven here and there before we would work. . . .

From these American students we Nigerians can learn a great lesson. Whatever our position may be, we must not think too high to do dirty work like road-making.

The way they worked surprised me, because I have never seen white people working like that before.

For the first time, then, young members of the African elite are presented with this different picture of what is "modern, rich, educated." Obviously, the picture is a propaganda poster rather than an accurate portrait of America; the Americans are a selected group of young people dedicated to what they are doing for a limited time (a summer for Crossroads, two years for the Peace Corps). But this is irrelevant to their impact on the Africans. Obviously, also, that impact is fleeting, for the Americans soon leave while the Africans stay on in their elite environment. But they do no harm, and for a brief time, the Africans have been exposed, in the words of the first Nigerian student, to that "sense of responsibility" so lacking in the African elite. How many forms of aid can claim so much?

Not all conventional foreign aid in Africa is useless or harmful. Foreign doctors and medicines save African lives. Foreign engineers and machines build roads. But whatever good aid does must be balanced against the prolonging of African dependence—both financial and spiritual—on the outside world. An example cited earlier is American surplus food: it feeds the hungry but it also has a depressing effect on local food production and probably government initiative. It might be possible to devise forms of aid, usually in modest quantities, that would not have such bad effects. But this seems hardly likely to happen in the context of cold-war competition and the attitudes that most foreigners bring to Africa.

When aid does come under criticism abroad, it is usually for quite different reasons. Senator Wayne Morse has led a growing Congressional attack on U.S. aid, but he seems concerned primarily with waste and lack of political results. The African leaders have shown that, thanks to the cold war, they can extract aid without becoming satellites (except perhaps for some of France's remaining client–states). When the Russians showed signs of reducing their aid to Africa, it was doubtless because they had failed—especially in Guinea—to get the political results they expected; it is hard to believe that they were concerned with the harm they did in Guinea. In France, the journalist Raymond Cartier of *Paris-Match* has given his name to a rebellion against de Gaulle's heavy spending in Africa. The *cartieristes* argue that the money would be better spent in France on useful projects than wasted on corrupting the elite in Africa, since the African nations will slip out of the French orbit eventually anyhow. But their concern is with France, not with Africa.

The subtle problems of aid and development escape most foreigners in Africa because they are still imbued with the confident arrogance of the missionary. The missionary himself, carrying his alien and rigid faith to people who need a lot, but not him, is no more than a parody of common foreign attitudes in Africa. Of several encounters with missionaries, I recall particularly an attempt to get information from an American evangelist in Portuguese Guinea. Information was hard to come by, and the American had spent five years in a particularly interesting corner of the country. I asked if there had been any economic development in his area during those years. "There can be no development," he intoned. "Eh?" I said. He repeated his phrase, and I had to say that I did not understand what he meant. "There can be no development," he explained, as if to an idiot, "because these people do not have the Lord." I left soon after.

This is manifestly silly, but the thinking of many of the foreign experts who throng to Africa is not very different. "There can be no development," these new missionaries say, "until these people have our way of life, our political system, our schools, or our economic system." In each case, they want the Africans to swallow whole their methods, their techniques, their culture. Even the specifically religious theme—"the Lord"—creeps into the thinking of some specialists. An American example is George H. T. Kimble. In *Tropical Africa* he writes of:

> . . . the idealism of those who see in Christianity the answer to all that is base and debasing in indigenous African cultures. It is an idealism that has come to be shared by Africans as much as by non-Africans and is almost certainly the greatest single force for social change in tropical Africa. Christianity has no monopoly of social idealism, it is true, but it takes a strong brand of idealism to flourish in the African climate, and not even its harshest critics are disposed to doubt that Christianity is such a breed.

When discussing the Teita tribe of Kenya, Kimble is able to write that, in their traditional society, "the Teita are nothing if not egalitarian," and also to report that "on the positive side" of social change, "many of them have accepted the Christian view . . . of the brotherhood of man." Aside from the fact that this last principle was seldom practiced by those who brought it to Africa —many churches were segregated and the lesson in those churches was hardly "the brotherhood of man"—one wonders just what the author believes is the difference between "brotherhood of man" and the Teita's "egalitarian" society.

The "Lord" need not be Christian, as long as he is not African. In reviewing Kimble's book, F. Fraser Darling, a respected ecologist, states that "The greatest moral force in Africa has been Islam. This religion has done far more to stem the miasmic ooze of animism than any other. Kimble remarks how black Mohammedans think themselves better people than the pagans. Indeed they are, for the moral power of Islam affects every hour of their waking life." Earlier in his review, Darling points out accurately that agricultural technicians in Africa suffer from lack of scientific knowledge; he says that the colossal failure of the Tanganyika peanut scheme was due to lack of "ecological reconnaissance." The same is true of Darling. Where in Africa would Darling find evidence for his views on the "moral force" of Islam—in practice, not in the words of the Koran? Not in North Africa, where after a thousand years of Islam the exploitation of man by man was if anything greater than in Black Africa, with its "miasmic ooze of paganism"; not in such West African Muslim sects as the Murids; nor, certainly, would either Kimble or Darling find much support in the destructive record of the Christian and Arab slave trades.

So axiomatic, apparently, is the belief of such people

in the moral superiority of anything foreign to what is native to Africa that they need not bother to provide any evidence. It is here, in this unshakable sense of superiority, that lies the fault with the work that so many foreigners do in Africa, no matter how good their intentions. Since their methods—religious, political or economic—are clearly better, there is no reason for them to know anything about Africa. And so Africa is the continent of the instant expert—a couple of hours after he gets off the plane, he starts telling the Africans what to do. If he is an agricultural "expert," his knowledge of African soils may be so inadequate that he will attempt to introduce techniques designed for a different environment, and seldom indeed does he know—or feel that he should know—anything about how agriculture fits into the complex web of traditional society. At an open-air meeting in the bush, I listened to a young technician from the West Indies outline to an African audience an ambitious, and in my opinion impossible, plan for regrouping peasant populations. Afterward I questioned him about it. "I have very fixed ideas," he declared. He had been in Africa one month.

When in 1963 the Senegalese government asked for U.S. aid for an agricultural project, an American official was sent to study their proposal and its background. His report covered nine major questions, including the "receptiveness of Senegalese farmers," and passed judgment on the *animation rurale* movement described in Chapter Six. His subject was nothing less than the entire organization of agricultural extension work in Senegal. Yet in order to evaluate this organization, the American official had spent just two weeks in Senegal. In his report he admits that the time was too short for a "thorough study," but adds that "it is not likely that much vital additional information, which would materially affect the recommendations or conclusions presented here, would be collected over a longer period of time." Though many of his observations are sound, the American seems to have completely missed the point of *animation,* which is not surprising in a two-week visit. Obviously, neither he nor anyone else would consider it possible to tell France or Denmark how to organize their agriculture after two weeks of study. Yet the job is in many ways harder in Senegal, a nation of six major races where relatively little is known about either soils or agricultural techniques, and less about the social environment.

The Communist nations offer their agricultural advice with an even more sublime and unwarranted confidence. In Guinea, the Russians were willing to draw up a project for increasing rice production, though the Russians have little experience in tropical agriculture. The Guineans turned down the Russian proposal, which would have cost about ten times what an earlier French study estimated to be the maximum economic cost. Several of the Eastern European nations are inviting Africans to study agriculture in their schools. What, I wonder, do the Eastern Europeans think they have accomplished in agriculture that is worth teaching to anyone, including Africans? How, by a combination of Stalinism and incompetence, one can transform agricultural surpluses into deficits? Before World War I, Russia, and most other Eastern European nations, exported food; now they are buying food from the West. The sorry Communist record in agriculture, on which the most vocal authority used to be Nikita Khrushchev himself, hardly seems to qualify them as teachers.

If the country involved were not African, I doubt that the U.S. aid officials would have considered two weeks time enough to pass judgment on Senegalese agriculture. (In recent years, however, many of those involved in American aid operations have shown a much greater awareness of the baffling complexity of transferring technology from the U.S. to the underdeveloped world.) If the students were Western rather than African, I think even Khrushchev might have smiled at the idea of bringing them to Moscow to study a system of agriculture whose defects he found it impossible to overcome.

But no one laughs when these things happen in Africa. It is idle to expect any great improvement in foreign aid to Africa as long as the missionary attitude prevails, as long as it is assumed that any technique or technician from an industrial nation is superior to anything or anyone that is African.

CHAPTER TEN

Bourgeois Marxists in Their Ivory Tower

"YOU'RE THE CORRUPTORS and we're the ones you're corrupting," a student at the University of Dakar remarked to me one day. We were chatting about the many countries—West, East, in between—from which he could get full scholarships, though he was admittedly doing little studying at Dakar. "I'm really only pretending to be a student here," he said with a smile, "and all these countries are willing to pay me to go on pretending."

My friend's "you" was directed, not at me as an American, but to the rich white industrial nations of the north, which look so alike from an African perspective. Many other African students are in my friend's position, but few of those I met could admit it with such cheerful frankness.

In their plunge into postcolonial Africa, the Great Powers have made a special effort to win the university students. Everyone, and particularly the students themselves, assumes that today's students are tomorrow's cabinet ministers. In a small African state, with a tiny elite, a few dozen university graduates may equal one vote in the United Nations. So a great power, by offering students an education in which they will be exposed to the beauties of that power's way of life ("two-party system," "Marxism-Leninism," etc.), sees an opportunity to pick up an African client-state at a bargain-basement price. Because education is involved, this operation can wrap itself in the cloak of self-righteousness and can, at least in the United States, attract the help of many people whose generous motive is simply to help Africa. Firm in the knowledge that their universities are the best, few of those involved seem to be aware that transplanting African students abroad causes problems as great as those of transplanting foreign education to Africa.

Since the demand for African students is now so great, and the supply still limited, it has become relatively easy for an African with a degree from secondary school to get into a university abroad or a foreign-financed university in Africa, often with a full scholarship. According to his preference, a good student can pick and choose between the representatives of foreign powers beating the bush for students. His first choice is likely to be a university in the ex-colonial nations, Britain or France, which still have the most African students. Failing that, there is the African-American Institute man recruiting for the United States, and the Soviet Embassy's offer to send him to Patrice Lumumba University in Moscow. Then, further down the list of student preference, there are places for him in Communist China, in West or East Germany, the Eastern European Communist nations, Yugoslavia, Egypt and Israel—in all the nations that seek an ideological or diplomatic toehold in Africa.

How great will be the political dividends for the great powers from investing in students is by no means clear yet. If an African student is unhappy abroad, and he often is, he is likely to come home resenting the host nation and its ideology. Many an African has switched from one side of the Iron Curtain to the other during his university career. The new host nation promptly trumpets this as an ideological triumph. Usually, however, the student has left because of the enormous difficulties of adjusting to a new climate, strange food, a different culture and language, new ways of teaching; or perhaps because he is lonely, or just because a friend has told him the grass is greener on the other side of the curtain. Naturally the student has enough political sense not to give these reasons for his defection.

Certainly the Russians, and the other East European Communist nations, must be wondering if they are not actually doing themselves harm with their student policy. In 1963 and 1964, Moscow, Sofia and Prague were plagued with clashes between African students and Communist authorities. The Africans told delighted Western newsmen that they were victims of racism; the United States Information Agency seized eagerly on this evidence that Communists can be racists too. Doubtless there was racism, though it may have been at least partly xenophobia; but the resentment of the Africans by Communist students had other roots. In Sofia, in Moscow, even in Belgrade, the African students are given scholarships that are far bigger than those of the local students; in some cases they get much more than the wage on which a working man supports his family. And since they are there for purely political reasons, the Africans are subjected to virtually no academic discipline. The Communist student, who is living on next to nothing, observes that the Africans have the time and money to take girls to cafés that he cannot afford. These Africans, better dressed than he and carrying transistor radios, do not look a bit like the people he had visualized as groaning, half-naked and in chains, under the heel of colonialism. The reasons for the Communist student's resentment are obvious. But the African student is not happy either. The reality of Moscow is pretty grim after the vision he had been given in Africa (a thought that seems never to occur to the Russians). The cold is dreadful, the food is unfamiliar, and, perhaps worst of all, the introverted people have none of the warmth and easy companionship of Africa. Instead of being grateful, as the Communist students feel they should be, the Africans react with remarks like this (from a Guinean): ". . . they [the Russians] haven't learned to behave like civilized people. They're just a bunch of peasants who've somehow learned to make a police state and a hydrogen bomb." In this context, the clashes between Africans and Communists are inevitable.

In the United States, the affluent American student has little reason to resent the African; more than elsewhere, too, there are Africans in the U.S. who have a hard time making ends meet. The United States also has the advantage of its decentralized university system. Certainly some Africans slide through without the effort required of Americans, as do other foreign students, but the private American university is in a better position than, say, Lumumba U., to treat an African as a student rather than as a pawn of governmental policy.

When they go abroad on what are really political scholarships, the African students' education is likely to suffer. All would be well, some seem to feel, if the students went to African universities instead. But there they are almost as far from "home," almost as alienated from the realities of Africa, as if they were at Lumumba U. or Ohio State. The university, whether it be in Nigeria or Madagascar, Senegal or Kenya, is copied literally after a European model. At the University of Ghana, professors and students wear gowns in British style, though the buildings look like California, and "classics" means Greece, not ancient Africa. "They want Harvard stone by stone," an American professor commented on a Nigerian university project. Some African studies have been added to the curriculum, but the spirit of the university is entirely that of another culture, in another century sometimes, facing different needs, so that what the student gets is largely irrelevant.

In some African nations, university scholarship policy helps separate the student from his environment. At the French-operated University of Dakar, the African student, surrounded by poverty, is better off than a European student. He receives a French scholarship of sixty dollars a month, plus from twenty to sixty dollars a month from his own government. After the student pays all his fees and room and board, he has left, as spending money, more than the wages on which a laborer supports a family; some students save more each month than the minimum monthly wage. So it is hardly surprising that some African students switch departments in an effort to prolong their pleasant university life.

Africa's rulers are more interested in building a university, which is a prime status symbol, than a secondary school. So while the foreign powers continue to lure away students, this continent of illiteracy is in the absurd position of having more university capacity than it can fill. In 1963 there were some two hundred empty seats at Makerere in Uganda, Dakar was little more than half full, and Nigeria was building universities that it will not need for a generation (if then). All over Africa new universities are being planned or are under construction. High scholarships, high costs of building and of hiring foreign professors, low enrollments—the per-student cost of university education in Africa is high indeed. In attempting to fill their universities, some governments have talked of keeping their students at home. But the men from the African-American Institute and Lumumba U. are still recruiting; and there is naturally more status to studying abroad than in Africa.

The importance of the present generation of university students to Africa's future hardly needs to be emphasized. The great powers may be wrong in assuming that they will be tomorrow's rulers, but they should be the artisans of social and economic change. They should be the innovators who will design a new Africa in which peasants and rulers will once more belong to the same society. The students themselves, and some other optimistic Africans, believe that they, the new elite, will clean up the mess made by the present rulers. Yet the circumstances of their education, abroad or in Africa, seem designed to prevent them from carrying out their tasks, to produce men who cannot measure up to the challenge of shaping Africa's future. The students are corrupted both by foreigners and by their elders in the elite.

African students are "radical." This is the conventional assumption. Western authorities worry about what will happen when the students come to power, and a U.S. government circular, proposing studies of the next generations of the elite, returns like a dog to his bone to the supposed radicalism of the students. As long as cold-war ideological standards are applied, there is plenty of evidence that the students are indeed radical. Student organizations—notably those in Paris and Dakar —proclaim a pro-Communist point of view. It is fashionable for African students to be against their governments, and they usually say they are to the "left" of the rulers. When you ask a student about his politics, a common answer is: "I am a Marxist-Leninist."

But when the students are looked at in African terms, the radicalism of most of them dissipates in hot air. The proclaimed Marxist-Leninist is, in his behavior, supremely bourgeois. His real interests are not the reading of Marx and Lenin, but the acquiring of natty clothes, transistor radios and cars or motor bikes. Student opposition to African governments is mainly oratorical. Like everyone else, students attack corruption. They are vociferous in their criticisms of "neocolonialism" and foreign military bases in Africa, issues that are safe, since they do not cut to the heart of present-day African problems. When it comes to the position of the elite, its excessive privileges and its monopoly of political power, its discrimination against the peasant population—the students are generally silent. "Help for the peasant masses," students may say, but they do not demand the drastic reduction in elite power that such help requires. Certainly they do not demand a reduction in their own privileges. They are able, in fact, to seek an increase in those privileges while denouncing the waste in the government. When I asked the president of the Senegalese Student Union about their grievances, he divided them into two categories. In Senegalese politics, he said, the students criticize ministers who live high on the hog. In student affairs, he went on, the union wants an increase in scholarships. It costs a dollar, he complained, to take a taxi from the university to downtown Dakar (bus

service is available). Student strikes for better living conditions are familiar in African universities and secondary schools.

A curiously unreal quality permeates student talk
about their government and their nation. They know a
lot about elite politics, and something (not much) about
Marx and Lenin, but little about what is going on outside the capital, nor do they seem interested in finding
out. In 1962 the Senegalese government offered to take
a group of students home on vacation from Paris—they
were self-proclaimed leftist critics of the government—
on a tour of rural development projects. It was, for the
students, an excellent opportunity to find out what the
government was, or was not, doing for those "peasant
masses." On the appointed day, not a single student
showed up; all were too busy to make a hot and uncom-
fortable tour in the bush. At a café in Paris some months
later, a student told me his version of the story. After the
students failed to appear, a Senegalese official said to
him: "You claim to be in the opposition, but you are
not serious people." The student grinned and shrugged.
"I suppose he was right," he admitted. He then told me
that he was planning to go to New York—to research a
thesis on rural reform in Senegal. We both smiled, he a
bit sheepishly.

In fact, students and governments have a great deal in
common. Both believe in rule by the educated elite, and
therefore neither really questions the privileged position
of ministers or students. It would be suicidal for the
students to attack the system whose privileges they expect to inherit. As a result, however loud their opposition in the student halls, they usually pass on graduation
right into the Establishment and gratefully accept their
villas and their Mercedes. Their quarrels with the re-

gime are usually a matter of jobs, of who gets what; quarrels that do not threaten the system itself. Here the students face a problem that may soon become acute. Most of the good jobs are taken, usually by young men who will be in office for many years to come, yet the supply of graduates is increasing rapidly. Soon Africa may suffer from that strange paradox found already in Egypt, India and Latin America: widespread illiteracy, and unemployment among university graduates. African politics then might become a fight for jobs between elite cliques. Today's students are understandably bitter, as they see they cannot hope to rise as fast or as far as their predecessors.

Still, the students, like the elite itself, are influenced by ideals of social justice. Neither callous nor ignorant, the students would like to see themselves as revolutionaries dedicated to modernizing their continent— though they also want the privileges to which they have become accustomed. Though they know they are in fact kept men while studying abroad, they want Africa to be truly independent. Their loose brand of "Marxism-Leninism" provides a convenient solution for these contradictions. Communist doctrine calls for a small governing elite, and Soviet practice has long abandoned any pretense at economic as well as political equality. (Sékou Touré noted that elite theory was used by his pro-Communist opponents in an effort to create what he called "a privileged caste.") Attacks on neocolonialism (but not on renouncing African in favor of foreign thinking) have the proper ring of independence. Best of all, the Communist opposition to "reformism" makes it possible to sound revolutionary without doing anything for Africa that involves work.

One of many examples of student revolutionary sloth

occurred in Paris during the winter of 1962–3. A pathetic sight that winter, the harshest in many years, was the hundreds of African laborers shivering in cotton pants and tee-shirts; these Africans, whose numbers have greatly increased in recent years, are generally illiterate and unskilled, so they are either unemployed or hold the most menial jobs. Jean-Pierre N'Diaye, the African sociologist, published an appeal in *Le Monde* for old clothes for the laborers. The French public responded with forty tons of clothing. Then N'Diaye asked African students to help him pass out the clothes. "One hour a week for Africa," he asked. Of the twenty-five hundred African students in Paris, exactly one volunteered, and he was a childhood friend of N'Diaye. The student union, the Fédération des Etudiants d'Afrique Noire en France, influenced by the elderly Stalinoid fossils of the French Communist Party, actively opposed N'Diaye's project on the grounds that it was "reformism" which, by improving the lot of the working class, would serve to delay the "revolution."

The students, therefore, can have the best of both worlds: revolutionaries who live the easy life. Foreigners encourage these attitudes by the extraordinary importance they attach to African students. I doubt if students in any other culture are so often surveyed, invited to give their opinions on any subject and listened to with outward respect by foreigners who would hardly listen to students of their own nationality. In 1961–2, both the French Communist Party and the U.S. Central Intelligence Agency apparently had agents at the University of Dakar (full-time foreign agents, not part-time local employees). I have no proof, but I doubt if either organization made a proportionate effort to observe other sectors of Senegalese society.

His experience abroad is likely to corrupt the student
in other ways. Since he is aware that he is there for political rather than academic reasons, he may grow lazy
and drift through his time, knowing full well that no
one is going to expel him for scholastic failure. This is
probably more true in Eastern Europe than elsewhere,
but there have been such cases in the U.S. too. Living in
a glamorous industrial society, whether or not he is
well off himself, the student's taste for bourgeois living
is whetted, but not necessarily his productivity; the
wealth around him is more visible than the attitudes
that produced it.

Like his elders who went to European schools, the
student is alienated from the traditional society of
Africa. Despite outward braggadocio, his sense of inferiority toward Europeans is likely to be deepened; he
knows he is not competing on equal terms with non-
African students. Jean-Pierre N'Diaye's 1961 survey of
African student opinion in France, based on interviews
with 310 students selected at random, provides fascinating insights into student thinking. A striking case of
dependence on Europe is Question 42: Do you think
Africa needs foreign aid to develop its economy? Of the
fifty questions in the survey, only this one got a unani-
mous response—all 310 students replied "yes." The
answer may be accurate, or at least realistic; but it
seems significant that, among all 310 young men, not
one was fiery or determined enough to say that Africa
could go it alone. Almost half (46 per cent) thought the
elite should be trained abroad; only one-third thought
they should be educated in Africa. When asked to pass
judgment on their fellow students, the Africans' main
criticism was "individualism" (as opposed to traditional
African solidarity of the community), followed by "not

aware of their responsibilities," "vanity," "Occidental-
ized." The theme of European influence runs through
the comments the students added to their responses:

> Snobs, stupidly taking on the indifference and in-
> dividualism for which we criticize the French.

> Unfortunately they've lost African dignity. It seems
> to me they are not proud of the color of their skin.

> . . . doubtless all this is to "ape" the whites . . .

> Those guys, don't even mention them to me! The
> worst colonialists of all are being turned out . . .

When I met N'Diaye, two years after his survey, he
was greatly concerned about the alienation of Africans
abroad. "We suffocate here," he said. He found his
fellow Africans crushed under the weight of Europe.
" 'The whites are too strong for us,' they say." N'Diaye
said the Africans were incredulous when he told them
he had published his survey, *Enquête sur les Etudiants
Noirs en France,* and started a magazine of his own,
without "European" support. The students' surprise is
understandable, in view of the performance of their
union, the FEANF, which simply stopped publishing its
magazine when the French government cut off its subsidy in 1960; in 1964 it still had not reappeared.

Tempted by indolence, lacking in self-confidence,
alienated from Africa, these students are not promising
material when they leave school. If their views of Africa
are unreal, it is a natural product of the unreal isolation
of the university. The elite atmosphere in their government is all too similar to that abroad or in an African
university. Exposed to a European standard of living,

they demand the same standard at home. The reluctance of returning students to work outside the capital, where European-style living is centered, is well known. The student may have learned something abroad, but—in his enervating environment—he did not learn nearly as much as he could have. His productivity, after he goes home, will be far less than it should be. If foreign powers pay for his university education, either at home or abroad, it is Africa that pays the European salary he demands for the rest of his working life. For its university graduates, as for its whole system of education, Africa pays a high price indeed.

Obviously, there are exceptions, both among the students and among those who have already returned to Africa. Many students do well even when it is not required of them; and many, like my friend in Dakar, are at least aware of what is happening to their generation. A surprising number of the returning graduates are productive and energetic, often against great odds. And when the students do sink into idleness or corruption, it is of course not their fault—they are victims of a world they never made. But, as a group, the new elite looks remarkably like the men now in power. Speaking of the students' alienation, an African official commented: "If neocolonialism is being dominated by foreign influences, then these students are the most neocolonial of all Africans. I doubt if they will be much help to us." Some Africans even suspect that the net effect of university education, as it is now offered to Africans, is to prolong the economic waste and psychological "colonization" that keeps Africa dependent on the outside world. The leader of a West African Muslim reform movement took this reasoning to this conclusion: "When I look at our students, I wonder sometimes if there isn't some sort of unspoken conspiracy among all of you—Russians, Americans and the rest—to keep us dependent on you by corrupting the youth that should be our next generation of leaders."

CHAPTER ELEVEN

A New Harmony

W HAT AFRICANS NEED TODAY—perhaps more than anything else—is a new conception of themselves: a new African culture. No one has stated the need more clearly than Aimé Césaire: "A true Copernican revolution must be imposed here. . . . So much is rooted in Europe. In all parties, in all spheres from the extreme right to the extreme left, there is the habit of doing for us, the habit of arranging for us, the habit of thinking for us; in short, the habit of contesting that right to initiative which is in essence the right to personality."

Africa does indeed need a new way of seeing the world and itself if it is to recapture that "right to personality," the absence of which lies behind so many of the present elite's failures. But what kind of Copernican revolution: around what sun will the new African culture turn? The foreigners, and many educated Africans, have no doubts. Africa, they say, has no choice but to abandon its traditional culture and adopt industrial civilization in one of its several prepackaged brands: Western European,

American, or Soviet. Any effort to cling to old African values is sentimentalism, they say; the transition may be painful, but the price of becoming modern–industrial is taking on the culture and values of the modern–industrial nations.

But even at best, the view that Africa must "Westernize" its culture is based on an overly simple view of the West's history. The fallacy is the belief that the industrial revolution is an escalator that everyone mounts in the same place, and that Africa, therefore, must go through all the phases of the Western experience. In fact, Africa will mount the industrial escalator at a much higher level of technology. This has profound social implications. Africa will industrialize at a time when automation is already far advanced. It is nonsense to suppose that Africa will go through the nineteenth-century stage, when industry needed a great deal of labor. In Africa as in Pittsburgh, automated industry is cheaper. The beginnings of industry in Africa have already shown that the latest technology—using many machines and few men—is the most profitable. The FRIA bauxite mine in Guinea is an example; when you look at this fantastic series of machines, digging and processing the earth, you see that the few humans around are there in a secondary capacity, to service the machines when they need it. The point is that there is no reason to suppose that Africa will *ever* experience full employment, no matter how much industry it has. Factories will *never* absorb the young men flowing into the cities. On the contrary, it is likely that Africa will go directly from the underemployment of an agricultural economy to the unemployment of automation.

Yet the culture the industrial nations are exporting to Africa, under one guise or another, is based largely on the possibility of full employment. We are exporting (and educating toward) a goal of personal achievement: a person is measured by what he produces. (The uglier aspects of this highly competitive, individualistic way of life were summed up by Leo Durocher in his famous dictum: "Nice guys finish last"—a statement profoundly in contradiction with traditional African values.) But in a society where machines, not men, do the work, it is both cruel and pointless to use productivity as the measure of a man. Even in the United States, as Americans look toward an automated future, voices are being raised against what we call the Protestant ethic: Americans will have to recast their culture, their notion of what is "good" and "bad," once it is clear that work is not available for all. Yet in an absent-minded way, the industrial nations continue to export to Africa cultural values that, like surplus food, are no longer needed at home. This odd lapse in time is characteristic of the European relationship with Africa: it reminds one of a colonial Europe which self-seekingly, nostalgically, shipped to Africa a feudal system that had largely vanished from Europe itself.

The ambiguities involved in the clash between industrial and African values are clear in the case of the family system. One traditional custom that has been carried over virtually intact into the elite is "family solidarity," also known (particularly among foreigners) as "family parasitism" or, as the American economist Elliot Berg puts it, "organized free-loading." It is traditional society's form of social security—the collective consumption by a kinship group that takes place in the African village. Family solidarity requires anyone with an income to feed and shelter any member of his extended family, which numbers in the hundreds, for it includes distant cousins as well as brothers and sisters (even they, in a polygamous society, are likely to be plentiful). The distant relative who asks for food and shelter cannot be refused except at the price of great family and social disapproval.

The elite with their high incomes are obvious targets of the family system, and the results are visible whenever you visit an African official at home. His house and the compound around it are swarming with people who are, at first, difficult to place in the scheme of things. They do not seem to be servants, yet they are not equals; they greet the visitor but they do not join in the conversation. They are members of the official's vast family who have come to live with him at his expense, attracted by the lights of the city as well as by his income. Even city dwellers with modest incomes attract relatives from the bush. In the development in Dakar where we lived, there was a bus driver up the street who lived in one large room with wife and children—and relatives. He earned about a hundred dollars a month. Yet he had no less than sixteen relatives living with him, and only two of them were employed. He said it was impossible for him to make ends meet: "I buy a hundred-kilo sack of rice at the beginning of the month, when I'm paid, but it seems to be gone in no time . . ." He was discouraged from working harder by the realization that any increase in his income would simply attract more relatives.

The retarding effects of this system are obvious. Saving and investment are discouraged; corruption and nepotism and padded payrolls are encouraged. Austerity is made still more difficult. The cost of government rises; the state, like the individual, finds it hard to save and invest.

The useful aspects of family solidarity are less often recognized than the bad. Most simply, it keeps alive people who might otherwise be entirely destitute, if not starving—there is virtually no other social security in Africa. And it is an extremely efficient method of draining off some of the excessive income of the elite for the benefit of those who need it most; it is not perfect, but it may well be more effective than would be any other system of distribution in today's Africa. (In Conakry, capital of Guinea, the American AID mission had its office by the port. When a ship carrying American surplus rice came in, the Americans could watch from their window as trucks belonging to government officials hauled the rice off to their homes before it could enter official distribution channels. In discussing this sight, a young American diplomat commented with rare perception: "This is the fastest system of distribution you can have in this country. It gets the rice out to the people who need it." In government warehouses, the rice might simply rot away or be black marketed, perhaps abroad; but from the officials' homes it rapidly finds its way into the stomachs of their many kinsmen.) In a less obvious sense, family solidarity helps to bridge the cultural gap of Africa, for the alienated, Europeanized member of the elite is kept in constant personal contact with his uneducated relatives; he cannot entirely escape traditional Africa, and, through his relatives, he may have an indirect effect on the village from which they (and he) came.

Most important in the long run is the role the family system can play in the Africa of the future. The obvious social danger of automation is that it will produce a great gulf between the highly skilled who have jobs, and the unskilled jobless, even if these latter are supported in bread-and-circuses fashion. That gulf would be far more painful in a society where the unemployed are downgraded as human beings than in traditional Africa. What could be more relevant to automation than the African family system, with one skilled person maintaining a horde of relatives who are not considered failures simply because the economy does not provide jobs for them? If men are measured by their relations to other men, rather than by their productivity, then both the unemployed and the employed Africans can be "good" people in a sense that is impossible in our culture. The skilled man may have more privileges, but he cannot consider himself "superior" just because he has a job.

Traditional African culture is decaying, however, and many of its values are unsuited to the future. If Africa has its "Copernican revolution," if it works out a single culture encompassing both the elite and the peasants, that culture is likely to be a blend of African and foreign elements. The outline of that possible new Africa can be dimly seen in the thoughts of today's leaders.

We can at least see what they would *like*, whether or not they will achieve it. First of all, that new culture, by restoring faith in Africa itself, would mute the note of self-hatred so strong now in the writings of the elite, as, for example, in the Nigerian poet Wole Soyinka's picture of the African in London looking forward to the privileges he will have when he goes home:

> . . . *thinking of the government house,*
> *senior service car*
> *and hordes of admiring women awaiting me,*
> *Where the one-eyed man is king.*

The new Africa would be a place in which the elite would not describe themselves as one-eyed kings; the need for pride, for an African faith to follow, crops up again and again in African writing and conversations. A single culture would make communications possible between elite and peasants. Only then can technological change reach the villages. From Western culture, Africa would adopt the attitude of problem-solving, which in turn is based on the confidence that man can master his environment. Techniques would then be flexible and based on experience, not on rigid and meaningless bureaucratic rules (as in the elite now), nor on religion (as in traditional Africa). Much of the new Africa's political and social life would be based on the past. Julius Nyerere speaks of applying the family system to the nation, of widening, in effect, the web of relationships of village Africa to include a greater community than that of kinship. Many African leaders see the ideal political system as a large-scale version of the village palaver. Senghor has said: "Democracy is the application, on the national scale, of the method of palaver, of dialogue, which guides the life of our villages . . . discussion which makes possible decision on a line of conduct, applicable to all, accepted and respected by all. . . . He who has the mission of applying decisions thus made holds his mission from the people of the village collectively, who can, if he fails, withdraw their confidence. That is how Senegal has lived for centuries." Sékou Touré, who speaks of politics in the same vein, would go on to apply democracy within the family by raising women and youth from their present low status. (Since women do most of the work, it may well be that new methods would be more easily adopted by them than by their husbands.) In contrast to the reality of unchecked elite rule, Nyerere, Senghor and Touré all envision a system that has the essence of democracy: responsibility to (and of) the people. Like the traditional African chiefs, the elite would then be forced to respond to the will of rural Africa: they would no longer try to impose mock-European status symbols on the villagers. Rural Africa would then begin to adopt new techniques responding to its desires at a harmonious pace, fitting technology to society, as in the past, rather than society to technology. With human goals uppermost, Africa might achieve material prosperity without paying the price in the misery of Stalinism or laissez-faire capitalism. And the kind of schools Africa needs would grow naturally out of that new culture. Once imitation of Europe is banned from the schools, students need not go on mindlessly memorizing empty phrases and seeing as the summit of their ambitions a petty clerkship in an office. With pride in their land, they can take on the many tasks, none of them insoluble, that go into building a new Africa.

Africa could, in theory, adopt the technology of the industrial nations while retaining much of its own culture. In fact, if it is true that lack of self-respect, of pride in Africa, is the primary barrier to progress, it may be that the rejection of Western culture is necessary to the adoption of Western technology. Thus the exact opposite of the usual opinion—that Africa cannot have the techniques without the culture—may be correct. In this vein, the case of Japan is worth pondering. By far the most successful of non-Western nations in technology, Japan has suffered the least Western cultural influence. When a mission was sent to Europe in the nineteenth century to acquire European techniques, the Japanese stated that they wanted to get the technology without sacrificing their Japanese identity.

Such a blend would be easily accepted by African philosophy, which tends to be extremely flexible, and to value relationships more than fixed principles. Because of this flexibility, African culture has been able to survive under great stress. In the New World, where Indians died under the shock of enslavement, Africans managed to survive and maintain at least part of their culture. To the frustration of Europeans, Africans have often taken pieces of European culture and fitted them into their own framework. This is the meaning behind Mannoni's observation: "In general, it might be said that they accept everything in detail but refuse our civilization as a whole . . ." Churches have sprung up in Africa that combine Christian and traditional principles; much the same is true of Voodoo in Haiti. Just as is the case with the family system, some aspects of African philosophy seem relevant to current trends in the Western world. In its emphasis on the relative nature of truth, in its acceptance of apparent contradictions, African philosophy is closer to Einstein's universe than it is to the fixed mechanical universe of Newton.

This new African culture is still a dream, a vision toward which men are groping in the hopes of finding the keystone of a new society. Though it is a dream, it is not an impossible one. It will not come easily. Africa will go through more agonizing times like the present, when the short-run future looks bleak; but the troubles of today do not mean that tomorrow will never come. If that new day comes, if rural Africa can weave new patterns without destroying its social fabric, if the new African culture successfully reconciles human harmony (the African contribution) with material progress (the Western contribution), then Africa will have reason indeed for pride. "For," as Aimé Césaire wrote in 1939:

It's not true that the labor of man is done
that we have no more work in this world
parasites upon it
that all we need do is keep in step
The work of man is just begun . . .

Index

Index

216

DAVID HAPGOOD

David Hapgood was born in Petersham, Massachusetts, in 1926. He received his bachelor's degree in economics from Swarthmore College in 1947 and has since worked as a translator and newspaper reporter. For several years he wrote for *The New York Times* Sunday section, *The News of the Week in Review*. On a fellowship from the Institute of Current World Affairs for study in Africa, Mr. Hapgood lived in Senegal for a year, traveled throughout Africa for another, and returned to the States in 1963. Since then, as a part-time evaluator for the Peace Corps, he has made three trips to Africa evaluating Senegal, the Ivory Coast, Togo and Niger. A free-lance writer, Mr. Hapgood is also the author of *The Purge That Failed: Tammany vs. Powell,* a study of Congressman Adam Clayton Powell's 1958 election campaign, and of *Africa,* an upper elementary school text. He recently co-edited the report of the Massachusetts Institute of Technology conference on agriculture in the underdeveloped world. Mr. Hapgood lives in Princeton, New Jersey, with his wife and children.

DATE DUE

GAYLORD   #3523PI   Printed in USA

DEMCO